SHARON ELDER

Daily Devotional for Women 2025

365 Days of Inspiration to Start Your Day with Joy, Faith, and Purpose

First edition

This book was professionally typeset on Reedsy.
Find out more at reedsy.com

Contents

Introduction

Every day is a new gift from God, filled with opportunities to experience His love, grow in faith, and step into the unique calling He has for you. Life's journey is full of blessings, challenges, and lessons that shape us, and in each season, God offers strength, wisdom, and joy. Whether you're facing trials, celebrating victories, or simply navigating the routines of daily life, spending time in God's presence empowers you to live with purpose and joy.

This devotional is crafted to help you begin each day with a renewed heart, grounded in God's Word and encouraged by His promises. Every morning, you'll find inspiration to start your day centered on Christ, with themes that touch on all aspects of life—from building confidence and trusting God's timing to loving others and finding peace in His presence.

Each month of this devotional is organized around a theme that reflects the seasons of faith we all experience. You'll explore topics like:

- **New Beginnings** in January, starting the year with a heart open to God's plans
- **Embracing God's Love** in February, a month to reflect on His boundless love for you
- **Trusting in God's Timing** in March, surrendering control to His perfect plans

- **Renewal through Christ** in April, as we celebrate Easter and the gift of new life

Throughout this devotional, you'll encounter scripture that speaks directly to the needs of your heart, reflections that invite you into deeper understanding, and prayers that help you connect personally with God. Designed to be both comforting and challenging, these pages encourage you to step into the woman God created you to be, with boldness, joy, and an unshakable faith.

Additionally, you'll find special sections for times like Easter, Mother's Day, Thanksgiving, and Advent, bringing focused devotions for these seasons of celebration and reflection. These moments serve as spiritual markers throughout the year, inviting you to pause and honor the incredible story of God's love for us.

As you journey through these 365 days, remember that God meets you exactly where you are. You don't need to have everything figured out, nor do you have to walk alone. God is with you, guiding you through every step, offering His peace, wisdom, and grace. Whether you are just beginning your walk with Him or have journeyed with Him for years, my prayer is that this devotional will become a source of strength, a wellspring of joy, and a guide for living out His purpose each day.

May you draw near to God, discover His heart for you, and find inspiration to live each day with renewed joy, faith, and purpose. Welcome to this journey—a year filled with encouragement, growth, and God's unending love.

1

January

Week 1: Renewing Your Mind

Our minds are incredibly powerful. They shape how we see the world, how we respond to challenges, and how we live out our faith. In Romans 12:2, the apostle Paul gives us this crucial instruction: "Do not conform to the pattern of this world, but be transformed by the renewing of your mind. Then you will be able to test and approve what God's will is—His good, pleasing and perfect will."

As Christian women, we are called to think differently from the world around us. While the world often pushes us to prioritize appearance, success, and control, God calls us to think in ways that reflect His truth—truth that leads to peace, freedom, and spiritual growth. The process of renewing our minds allows us to shift our focus from the temporary pressures of life to God's eternal perspective.

January 1

The Power of Your Thoughts

"For as he thinks in his heart, so is he.

Proverbs 23:7

What you think about shapes who you become. If your thoughts are filled with worry, fear, and negativity, it's likely those things will take root in your life. However, when your thoughts align with God's truth—thoughts of love, peace, and trust—you will experience His transformative power. Today, ask yourself, "What thoughts have I been dwelling on?" Surrender any negative thoughts to God, and let Him fill your mind with His truth.

Reflect

How can I begin to replace negative thoughts with God's promises today?

January 2

Setting Your Mind on Things Above

"Set your minds on things above, not on earthly things."

Colossians 3:2

The busyness of life can pull our minds in many directions. Work responsibilities, family demands, and personal challenges often dominate our thoughts. Yet, God calls us to shift our focus upward—onto Him, His promises, and His eternal plans. Setting your mind on things above doesn't mean ignoring your responsibilities but rather seeing them through God's eyes. As you go through your day, practice turning your thoughts toward God and His goodness, allowing His perspective to guide you.

Prayer

Lord, help me to fix my thoughts on You today. In the midst of distractions, remind me to focus on Your truth and promises.

January 3

Taking Every Thought Captive

"We demolish arguments and every pretension that sets itself up against the knowledge of God, and we take captive every thought to make it obedient to Christ."

2 Corinthians 10:5

Our minds can sometimes be a battlefield, filled with doubts, fears, and anxieties. However, as believers, we have the authority in Christ to take control of these thoughts. Instead of letting them run wild, we can bring them under submission to the truth of God's Word. When negative or anxious thoughts arise, stop and ask yourself, "Is this thought aligned with God's truth?" If it's not, reject it and replace it with Scripture.

Reflect

What are some recurring negative thoughts in my life? What Scripture can I use to combat them?

January 4

The Mind of Christ

"Let this mind be in you, which was also in Christ Jesus."

Philippians 2:5

Having the mind of Christ means adopting His attitudes, values, and perspective. Jesus approached life with humility, compassion, and complete trust in the Father. As we renew our minds, we begin to think like Christ—to see others with love, to face challenges with faith, and to live with a spirit of humility. This transformation happens gradually, but it starts with a willingness to surrender our own thoughts and attitudes and ask God to give us the mind of Christ.

Prayer

Jesus, I want to think like You. Renew my mind so that I can adopt Your perspective and respond to life with grace and love.

January 5

Guarding Your Mind

"Above all else, guard your heart, for everything you do flows from it."

Proverbs 4:23

Guarding your heart and mind is essential in a world filled with distractions and temptations. What we consume through media, conversations, and even our environments can have a profound impact on our thoughts. Be mindful of what you allow into your mind—whether through social media, entertainment, or even the people you surround yourself with. Ask God for wisdom to protect your mind from anything that would pull you away from Him.

Reflection: What influences in my life are shaping my thoughts? Are they leading me closer to God, or further away?

January 6

Filling Your Mind with God's Word

"I have hidden Your word in my heart that I might not sin against You."

Psalm 119:11

The best way to renew your mind is by filling it with God's Word. His Word is living and active, and when we meditate on it, it transforms our thoughts, attitudes, and actions. Make it a priority to immerse yourself in Scripture daily. Whether through reading, listening, or memorizing verses, allow the truth of God's Word to shape your mind and direct your steps.

Prayer

Lord, help me to hunger for Your Word. Let it fill my mind and guide my thoughts, so I may be transformed by Your truth.

January 7

Renewed by God's Spirit

"You were taught... to be made new in the attitude of your minds; and to put on the new self, created to be like God in true righteousness and holiness."

Ephesians 4:23-24

The renewal of your mind is not something you can do on your own. It is a work of the Holy Spirit within you. As you open yourself to God, He begins to reshape your thoughts and attitudes. Each day, invite the Holy Spirit to renew your mind, helping you to think and live in ways that reflect God's love and purpose.

Reflect

In what ways do I need the Holy Spirit to renew my mind today?

Week 2: Trusting God's Plan

Trusting God's plan for your life can be one of the most challenging aspects of faith. When life feels uncertain, and the path forward is unclear, we may wonder where God is leading us. Yet, Scripture reminds us that God's ways are higher than our ways, and His plans for us are always good, even when we can't see the full picture. Trusting Him means believing that He is faithful and that He works all things for our good. This week, we'll explore what it means to place our trust in God's perfect plan, even when it doesn't make sense to us.

January 8

God's Plan is Good

"'For I know the plans I have for you,' declares the Lord, 'plans to prosper you and not to harm you, plans to give you hope and a future.'"

Jeremiah 29:11

One of the most comforting promises in the Bible is that God's plans for us are always good. Even when we face difficulties, disappointments, or detours, God is working behind the scenes for our ultimate good. His plans are not just for our present moment but for our future. Trust that in every season, God is preparing you for something greater. When you're tempted to doubt, remind yourself of His faithfulness and His promise to prosper you.

Reflect

Where in your life do you struggle to trust God's plan? How

can you remind yourself of His goodness today?

January 9

Lean Not on Your Own Understanding

"Trust in the Lord with all your heart and lean not on your own understanding; in all your ways submit to Him, and He will make your paths straight."

Proverbs 3:5-6

We often want to understand everything that happens in our lives. But sometimes, God's plan defies our logic and understanding. Trusting Him means letting go of the need to figure everything out and choosing to believe that He knows what's best. When we submit our ways to Him, He promises to make our paths straight, guiding us step by step. Today, release your need for control and trust in God's wisdom instead of your own.

Prayer

Lord, help me to trust You even when I don't understand. Guide my steps and give me peace in Your plan.

January 10

God's Timing is Perfect

"He has made everything beautiful in its time."

Ecclesiastes 3:11

One of the hardest parts of trusting God's plan is waiting for His timing. We often want things to happen quickly, but God sees the bigger picture and knows the perfect time for every event in our lives. His timing is not always ours, but it is always perfect. Whether you're waiting for an answered prayer, a breakthrough, or direction, trust that God is working behind the scenes to make everything beautiful in its time.

Reflect

What are you currently waiting on? How can you trust God's timing in this season?

January 11

Trusting Through Uncertainty

"The Lord is my strength and my shield; my heart trusts in Him, and He helps me."
Psalm 28:7

Life is full of uncertainties, and it's easy to feel overwhelmed when we don't know what the future holds. But even in times of uncertainty, God is our strength and shield. He is our protector, and He promises to help us when we place our trust in Him. When fear or doubt creeps in, remind yourself that God is in control, and nothing takes Him by surprise. He will give you the strength to face whatever comes your way.

Prayer

Lord, in times of uncertainty, help me to trust that You are my strength and protector. Calm my fears and help me rely on You.

January 12

Surrendering Your Will to God

"Father, if You are willing, take this cup from me; yet not my will, but Yours be done."
Luke 22:42

Even Jesus, in His moment of greatest trial, prayed for God's will to be done over His own desires. Trusting God's plan often requires us to surrender our own will and desires, even when we don't fully understand what He's doing. It's not always easy, but true trust means believing that God's way is better, even when it doesn't align with what we want. Today, practice surrendering your plans to God and asking for His will to be done.

Reflect

What areas of your life are hardest to surrender to God? How can you trust that His will is better than your own?

January 13

God's Plan Includes Peace

"You will keep in perfect peace those whose minds are steadfast, because they trust in You." Isaiah 26:3

When we trust in God's plan, peace follows. It doesn't mean that everything in life will go smoothly, but it does mean that we can experience God's perfect peace even in the midst of chaos. Keeping our minds steadfast—focused on God and His promises—helps us remain anchored in peace. Trusting God's plan means trusting that He is in control, even when life feels uncertain or overwhelming. Let His peace fill your heart today.

Prayer

Lord, help me keep my mind focused on You, trusting that Your plan brings peace to my soul.

January 14

Trusting in the Unknown

"Now faith is confidence in what we hope for and assurance

about what we do not see.
Hebrews 11:1

Faith is trusting in what we cannot see. It's believing in God's promises even when the path ahead is unclear. Trusting God's plan often requires stepping out in faith, even when you don't know the outcome. Just like Abraham, who obeyed God without knowing where he was going, we are called to walk by faith and not by sight. Trust that even in the unknown, God is leading you toward His good purposes.

Reflect

In what areas of your life are you being called to trust God with the unknown? How can you take a step of faith today?

Week 3: Casting Your Cares on Him

Life often brings burdens that can weigh heavily on our hearts—stress, worries, and anxieties that seem overwhelming. Yet, God invites us to bring all these cares to Him. In 1 Peter 5:7, we are reminded to "cast all your anxiety on Him because He cares for you." This week, we will focus on what it means to release our burdens to God and trust Him with our worries. Instead of carrying the weight of the world on our shoulders, we can rely on God's strength and care.

January 15

God Cares for You

"Cast all your anxiety on Him because He cares for you."
1 Peter 5:7

This simple yet profound verse is a beautiful reminder that God cares deeply about every detail of your life. He sees your struggles, your fears, and your worries, and He wants you to bring them to Him. Sometimes we may hesitate to burden God with our problems, but He invites us to cast every care onto Him. He is not distant or indifferent—He is a loving Father who is ready and willing to carry the weight of your anxieties.

Reflect

What cares or worries are you holding onto? Take a moment to release them to God, knowing He cares for you.

January 16

Letting Go of Control

"Be still, and know that I am God."

Psalm 46:10

One of the reasons we hold onto our burdens is the desire to control our circumstances. We think that if we worry enough or plan enough, we can fix everything. But God calls us to be still and trust in Him. Letting go of control doesn't mean we stop caring about the issues we face, but it does mean surrendering the outcome to God. Trusting Him with your cares means acknowledging that He is in control, not you, and that He can handle it better than you ever could.

Prayer

Lord, help me to let go of the things I'm trying to control. I trust You to take care of what I cannot.

January 17

His Yoke is Easy

"Come to Me, all you who are weary and burdened, and I will give you rest. Take My yoke upon you and learn from Me, for I am gentle and humble in heart, and you will find rest for your souls. For My yoke is easy and My burden is light."
Matthew 11:28-30

Jesus invites us to come to Him when we are weary and burdened. He offers us rest—not just physical rest, but rest for our souls. When we try to carry our burdens alone, we grow weary. But when we take His yoke upon us, we find that His way is gentle and His burden is light. He doesn't promise a life without challenges, but He does promise that we don't have to face them alone. In His strength, we find peace and rest.

Reflect

Are you feeling weary or burdened? Take Jesus up on His invitation and exchange your heavy burden for His light one.

January 18

Don't Worry About Tomorrow

"Therefore do not worry about tomorrow, for tomorrow will worry about itself. Each day has enough trouble of its own."
Matthew 6:34

Worry often comes from projecting into the future—thinking about all the "what ifs" and possible scenarios. But Jesus reminds us not to worry about tomorrow. God gives us the grace we need for today, and we can trust Him to provide for tomorrow when it comes. Worrying about the future only adds unnecessary stress to our lives. Instead, focus on what God is doing right now and trust Him with whatever comes next.

Prayer

Lord, help me to live in the present and trust You with tomorrow. I release my future worries into Your hands.

January 19

The Peace of God

"Do not be anxious about anything, but in every situation, by prayer and petition, with thanksgiving, present your requests to God. And the peace of God, which transcends all understanding, will guard your hearts and your minds in Christ Jesus."
Philippians 4:6-7

Anxiety can often feel overwhelming, but God gives us a clear way to deal with it—through prayer. When we bring our anxieties to God in prayer, and do so with a thankful heart, we open ourselves to receive His peace. This peace is not something we can manufacture on our own; it's a supernatural peace that goes beyond our understanding. It guards our hearts and minds, keeping us centered in Christ even when life feels chaotic.

Reflect

What are you anxious about today? Bring those worries to God in prayer, and ask Him for His peace to fill your heart.

January 20

God Will Sustain You

"Cast your cares on the Lord and He will sustain you; He will never let the righteous be shaken."
Psalm 55:22

When we cast our cares on the Lord, He doesn't just take them away—He sustains us. He gives us the strength and grace to face each day, no matter what challenges come our way. Trusting God with your burdens doesn't mean that life will be free of trials, but it does mean that He will be with you through them all, holding you up and giving you what you need to endure. Rest in the promise that God will sustain you as you release your cares to Him.

Prayer

Lord, thank You for sustaining me in every season. I trust You to carry me through whatever comes my way.

January 21

God is Your Refuge

"The Lord is a refuge for the oppressed, a stronghold in times of trouble."

Psalm 9:9

God is not only our burden-bearer, but He is also our refuge. In times of trouble, He is a safe place we can run to. When life feels overwhelming and burdens are too heavy to bear, we can find safety, comfort, and peace in His presence. Whatever challenges you face, know that God is your stronghold, your protector, and your shelter. You don't have to face life's storms on your own—God is with you, offering you refuge and strength.

Reflect

What burdens do you need to release to God today? Run to Him as your refuge, knowing He is ready to receive you with open arms.

Week 4: Finding Strength in God

Life's trials can sometimes feel overwhelming. Whether it's the weight of daily responsibilities, personal struggles, or unexpected hardships, we all face moments when we feel weak and drained. However, as believers, our strength is not found in ourselves but in God. He promises to be our source of strength, even when we feel like we can't go on. This week, we'll explore what it means to rely on God's strength rather than our own and how His power sustains us in every season.

January 22

God is Your Strength

"The Lord is my strength and my defense; He has become my salvation."

Exodus 15:2

In moments of weakness, remember that God is not just a helper—He *is* your strength. When you feel like you have nothing left to give, God steps in to empower you. He doesn't expect you to carry your burdens alone. Instead, He invites you to lean on Him, allowing His strength to sustain you. Today, surrender your weariness to God and allow His power to fill you with renewed strength.

Reflect

In what areas of your life do you need God's strength right now? Take time to invite Him into those areas today.

January 23

His Power is Made Perfect in Weakness

"But He said to me, 'My grace is sufficient for you, for My power is

made perfect in weakness.' Therefore I will boast all the more gladly about my weaknesses, so that Christ's power may rest on me."

2 Corinthians 12:9

It's often in our weakest moments that God's power shines the brightest. We may try to hide our weaknesses or feel embarrassed by them, but God works through them. His grace is enough to cover our weaknesses, and His power is made perfect when we surrender our struggles to Him. Rather than focusing on your limitations, embrace them as opportunities for God to show His strength in your life.

Prayer

Lord, thank You for using my weaknesses to reveal Your power. Help me to rely on Your grace and strength today.

January 24

Strength for Every Season

"I can do all this through Him who gives me strength."

Philippians 4:13

No matter what season of life you're in, whether it's a time of abundance or hardship, God is your source of strength. Paul wrote this verse while in prison, yet he declared that he could do all things through Christ. This doesn't mean that life will always be easy, but it does mean that God will give you the strength to face whatever comes your way. When you feel overwhelmed, remind yourself that Christ is your strength, and with Him, you can endure anything.

Reflect

What challenges are you facing right now? How can you rely on Christ's strength to help you through them?

January 25

Wait on the Lord

"But those who hope in the Lord will renew their strength. They will soar on wings like eagles; they will run and not grow weary, they will walk and not be faint."

Isaiah 40:31

When we feel weary, it's tempting to rely on our own efforts to push through. But Scripture teaches us that when we wait on the Lord, our strength is renewed. Waiting on God doesn't mean sitting idly; it means trusting Him, resting in His timing, and allowing Him to renew your spirit. When you feel like giving up, pause and wait on God. He promises to give you the strength you need to keep going.

Prayer

Lord, teach me to wait on You and trust in Your perfect timing. Renew my strength and help me rely on You instead of my own efforts.

January 26

The Joy of the Lord is Your Strength

"Do not grieve, for the joy of the Lord is your strength."

Nehemiah 8:10

There's a deep connection between joy and strength. The joy that comes from knowing God, trusting in His goodness, and experiencing His presence can strengthen us in ways that nothing else can. Even in difficult times, we can find joy in the Lord, and that joy becomes the strength we need to endure. Today, focus on the joy of knowing that God is with you, that He loves you, and that His plans for you are good. Let that joy fuel your strength.

Reflect

How can you cultivate the joy of the Lord in your life today? What are some ways you can shift your focus to God's goodness?

January 27

God's Strength in Times of Trouble

"God is our refuge and strength, an ever-present help in trouble."
Psalm 46:1

When trouble comes, we often feel shaken and vulnerable. But God is our refuge and strength—a safe place we can run to when life feels uncertain. He is ever-present, meaning He is always near and ready to help us in times of trouble. No matter what you're facing, God is with you. He is your protector, your fortress, and your strength. You don't have to face challenges alone; God is with you every step of the way.

Prayer

Lord, thank You for being my refuge and strength in times of trouble. Help me to trust in Your protection and lean on You when I feel overwhelmed.

January 28

Strengthened by His Spirit

"I pray that out of His glorious riches He may strengthen you with power through His Spirit in your inner being."
Ephesians 3:16

God strengthens us from the inside out through His Holy Spirit. His power is not just for the external challenges we face but for our inner being—our hearts, minds, and souls. As we rely on the Holy Spirit, we are empowered to live out our faith with boldness, courage, and perseverance. Today, invite the Holy Spirit to strengthen you in your inner being, giving you the power to face whatever lies ahead.

Reflect

How can you invite the Holy Spirit to strengthen you today? What areas of your life need His empowering presence?

January 29

God is Our Ever-Present Help

"God is our refuge and strength, an ever-present help in trouble."
Psalm 46:1

When we face challenges, it's easy to feel alone. Psalm 46 reminds us that God is not only our strength but our *ever-present* help. He is with us in every moment of our trials, offering protection, peace, and power beyond what we could ever muster on our own. Today, reflect on how God is both your refuge and your strength and allow Him to be your source of help in all things.

Reflect

Are there situations in your life where you're relying on your own strength instead of seeking God's help? Take a moment to bring these concerns to God, asking Him to be your strength.

Prayer

Lord, thank You for being my refuge and strength. Help me to rely on You in every challenge, knowing that You are always present to help me. Give me the courage to release control and to lean on You fully.

January 30

Strength in Our Weakness

"But He said to me, 'My grace is sufficient for you, for My power is made perfect in weakness.' Therefore I will boast all the more gladly about my weaknesses, so that Christ's power may rest on me." 2 Corinthians 12:9

Paul reminds us that God's strength shines brightest when we are weak. Instead of seeing our weaknesses as limitations, we can view them as opportunities for God's power to work through us. Our weaknesses are places where God can show up in remarkable ways, revealing His strength and grace in ways we might not experience otherwise. Today, embrace your weaknesses as spaces for God's power to rest upon you.

Reflect

What are some weaknesses you struggle with? How can you surrender these to God and allow His power to work through them?

Prayer

Lord, thank You for using my weaknesses to show Your strength. Help me to remember that Your grace is sufficient for me. When I feel weak, remind me that Your power is made perfect in my surrender.

January 31

Renewing Our Strength in the Lord

"But those who hope in the Lord will renew their strength. They will soar on wings like eagles; they will run and not grow weary, they will walk and not be faint."

Isaiah 40:31

When we place our hope in the Lord, He renews us with strength that endures. Like an eagle soaring high above, God enables us to rise above our circumstances, giving us the energy to persevere even when we feel drained. Hoping in the Lord is an active trust—a decision to believe that He will sustain us through all things. Today, place your hope in God and allow Him to renew and restore your strength.

Reflect

What areas of your life feel weary? How can you actively place your hope in the Lord, trusting Him to renew your strength?

Prayer

Lord, I put my hope in You today. I ask for Your strength to carry me through the challenges ahead. Renew my energy, my focus, and my spirit as I trust in You, knowing that You will sustain me through every season.

2

February

Week 1: Understanding God's Love for You

The foundation of our faith begins with understanding the depth of God's love for us. This love is not conditional, nor is it something we need to earn; it is freely given. God's love is perfect, eternal, and beyond anything we could ever imagine. This week, we will focus on exploring the nature of God's love, learning how to receive it, and discovering how His love changes everything about how we live our lives. Understanding God's love is the key to trusting Him, surrendering to Him, and finding peace and joy in His presence.

February 1

God's Love is Unconditional

"But God demonstrates His own love for us in this: While we were still sinners, Christ died for us."

Romans 5:8

One of the most incredible truths about God's love is that it is unconditional. He loved us before we even knew Him, before we could ever earn or deserve His love. While we were still lost in our sin, God sent Jesus to die for us as the ultimate expression of His love. We don't have to clean ourselves up or meet certain standards to receive this love. It's given freely, simply because God loves us as His children.

Reflect

How does knowing that God's love for you is unconditional change how you view your relationship with Him?

February 2

You Are His Beloved

"See what great love the Father has lavished on us, that we should be called children of God! And that is what we are!"

1 John 3:1

God not only loves you, but He calls you His beloved child. As a loving Father, He delights in you, cares for you, and wants to be in a close relationship with you. His love isn't distant or impersonal; it's intimate and personal. He knows you by name and sees you as His precious daughter. No matter what you've been through or how you see yourself, God sees you as beloved and cherished.

Prayer

Father, thank You for calling me Your beloved. Help me to embrace my identity as Your daughter and live in the truth of Your love.

February 3

Nothing Can Separate You from His Love

"For I am convinced that neither death nor life, neither angels nor demons, neither the present nor the future, nor any powers, neither height nor depth, nor anything else in all creation, will be able to separate us from the love of God that is in Christ Jesus our Lord."
Romans 8:38-39

God's love is constant and unshakable. No matter what happens in life—whether it's trials, suffering, or even our own mistakes—nothing can separate us from the love of God. This love is secure and eternal, anchored in Christ's sacrifice on the cross. When you feel distant from God or overwhelmed by life's challenges, remind yourself that God's love for you remains unchanged. You are always held in His loving embrace.

Reflect

In what situations do you feel distant from God? How can you remind yourself that His love is always with you?

February 4

Love that Casts Out Fear

"There is no fear in love. But perfect love drives out fear, because fear has to do with punishment. The one who fears is not made perfect in love."
1 John 4:18

God's perfect love is the antidote to fear. When we understand how deeply we are loved by Him, fear loses its grip on our hearts. We don't have to be afraid of the future, of failure, or of anything life throws at us because we know that God is for us and His love will carry us through. Fear often comes from feeling unworthy or uncertain, but God's love assures us that we are fully accepted and secure in Him.

Prayer

Lord, help me to rest in Your perfect love and let go of any fears that hold me back. Remind me that Your love is stronger than my fears.

February 5

Love That Redeems

"But because of His great love for us, God, who is rich in mercy, made us alive with Christ even when we were dead in transgressions—it is by grace you have been saved."

Ephesians 2:4-5

God's love is a redeeming love. Even when we were spiritually dead because of our sins, God, in His mercy, brought us back to life through Christ. His love reaches into our brokenness, forgives our sins, and gives us a new start. No matter how far we've fallen, God's love has the power to redeem us, heal us, and restore us. His grace is sufficient, and His love is more powerful than any mistake we've made.

Reflect

What areas of your life need redemption? How can you allow God's love and grace to bring healing and restoration to those places?

February 6

Love that Leads to Transformation

"Therefore, if anyone is in Christ, the new creation has come: The old has gone, the new is here!"

2 Corinthians 5:17

God's love not only saves us but transforms us. When we fully receive His love, it changes us from the inside out. We are no longer defined by our past or our failures. In Christ, we are made new. God's love gives us a new identity, new purpose, and new life. As you continue to grow in your understanding of God's love, allow it to transform the way you think, the way you live, and the way you see yourself.

Prayer

Lord, thank You for making me a new creation in Christ. Help me to live in the reality of this transformation and to reflect Your love in everything I do.

February 7

Responding to God's Love

"We love because He first loved us."

1 John 4:19

God's love for us calls for a response. As we experience His love, our natural response is to love Him in return and to love others. The love we show others is a reflection of the love we have received from God. It's not something we muster up on our own but something that flows out of the deep well of His love for us. Today, think about how you can respond to God's love in your life by showing love to those around you.

Reflect

How can you actively respond to God's love this week? In what ways can you show love to others as a reflection of His love for you?

Week 2: Loving Others Through Christ

Jesus commanded us to love others just as He has loved us. But true, Christ-like love goes beyond our natural tendencies. It calls us to love in ways that challenge us, stretch us, and sometimes push us beyond what we feel capable of. This week, we will explore what it means to love others through the power of Christ's love in us. We'll learn how to show grace, compassion, and forgiveness, reflecting the love that Jesus has so freely given to us.

February 8

Love One Another as I Have Loved You

"A new command I give you: Love one another. As I have loved you, so you must love one another."
John 13:34

Jesus set the standard for how we are to love others—by loving them as He has loved us. His love is selfless, sacrificial, and unconditional. He loves us despite our flaws and imperfections, and He calls us to love others in the same way. Loving others through Christ means seeing them through His eyes, with compassion and grace, and serving them as He has served us. It is a love that goes beyond our natural capacity, empowered by His Spirit.

Reflect

Who in your life needs to experience Christ's love through you? How can you demonstrate that love today?

February 9

The Power of Forgiveness

"Be kind and compassionate to one another, forgiving each other, just as in Christ God forgave you."
Ephesians 4:32

Forgiveness is one of the most powerful expressions of love. It's not always easy, especially when we've been hurt deeply, but Christ calls us to forgive others just as He has forgiven us. When we forgive, we release the weight of bitterness and make room for healing and restoration. It's through His strength, not our own, that we can extend grace to those who have wronged us. Forgiveness is an act of love that sets both the giver and receiver free.

Prayer

Lord, help me to forgive others as You have forgiven me. Give me the grace to let go of any bitterness and love with a heart full of compassion.

February 10

Loving the Difficult People

"But I tell you, love your enemies and pray for those who persecute you."
Matthew 5:44

Loving people who are kind and easy to get along with is relatively simple. But Jesus challenges us to go further by loving those who are difficult—even our enemies. This kind of love is radical and countercultural, but it reflects the heart of God. When we choose to love and pray for those who hurt or oppose us, we are allowing Christ's love to shine through us. It's not about excusing bad behavior, but about choosing love over hate and trusting God to work in their hearts.

Reflect

Is there someone in your life who is difficult to love? Ask God to help you love and pray for that person, trusting Him to do a work in both of your hearts.

February 11

Loving Through Serving

"For even the Son of Man did not come to be served, but to serve, and to give His life as a ransom for many."

Mark 10:45

Jesus modeled servant-hearted love throughout His ministry. He washed His disciples' feet, healed the sick, and ultimately gave His life for us. Loving others often means serving them, putting their needs before our own. When we serve others, we reflect the heart of Christ. Whether it's through small acts of kindness or large sacrifices, serving is one of the most practical ways we can show love. True love seeks to give, not to take.

Prayer

Lord, teach me how to serve others with the same humility and love that You've shown me. Open my eyes to opportunities to serve those around me today.

February 12

Love is Patient and Kind

"Love is patient, love is kind. It does not envy, it does not boast, it is not proud."

1 Corinthians 13:4

Paul's famous passage on love reminds us of the characteristics of true, godly love. It is patient and kind, even when others test our limits. It doesn't envy or seek its own glory, but it humbly lifts others up. Loving others through Christ means embodying these qualities in our daily interactions. It's easy to become impatient or frustrated with others, but when we allow God's love to fill us, we can respond with grace and kindness, even in difficult situations.

Reflect

How can you practice patience and kindness with those around you this week? In what ways can you reflect the characteristics of Christ-like love?

February 13

Bearing One Another's Burdens

"Carry each other's burdens, and in this way you will fulfill the law of Christ."

Galatians 6:2

Loving others means walking alongside them in their struggles. We are called to bear each other's burdens, offering support, encouragement, and prayer when life gets heavy. Whether it's offering a listening ear, providing practical help, or lifting someone up in prayer, bearing another's burdens reflects the love of Christ. Just as Jesus carries our burdens, we are called to do the same for others. This kind of love requires selflessness and compassion, but it brings healing and unity within the body of Christ.

Prayer

Lord, give me the heart to carry the burdens of those around me. Help me to show love by supporting and encouraging those who are struggling.

February 14

Love in Action

"Dear children, let us not love with words or speech but with actions and in truth."

1 John 3:18

True love isn't just about words—it's about action. Loving others through Christ means putting our love into practice in tangible ways. It's not enough to say we love someone; we must show it through our actions. This could mean acts of kindness, generosity, or simply being there for someone in their time of need. When we love through action, we reflect the love of Jesus, who didn't just speak of love but demonstrated it through His life and sacrifice.

Reflect

How can you put your love into action this week? Think of specific ways you can demonstrate Christ's love to those around you through practical acts of kindness.

Week 3: Healing from Hurt and Forgiveness

Hurt is an inevitable part of life. Whether it's caused by others, circumstances, or even ourselves, the pain of emotional wounds can linger. But God offers us healing through the power of His love and grace. Central to that healing is forgiveness—both receiving it and extending it. Forgiveness is not about excusing wrongdoing, but about freeing ourselves from the weight of bitterness and opening our hearts to God's restorative work. This week, we will explore the journey of healing from hurt and the power of forgiveness.

February 15

God Heals the Brokenhearted

"He heals the brokenhearted and binds up their wounds."
Psalm 147:3

When we are hurting, it can feel like no one truly understands the depth of our pain. But God does. He is not distant in our suffering but comes close to heal the wounds of our hearts. God's healing may not always come in the way we expect, but He promises to bind up our wounds, to restore our hearts, and to lead us into wholeness. Whatever pain you are carrying, know that God is your Healer. He sees your hurt, and He is ready to mend your heart.

Reflect

What hurts are you holding onto? Take time to bring them before God, trusting Him to heal your heart.

February 16

Forgiving as You've Been Forgiven

"Bear with each other and forgive one another if any of you has a grievance against someone. Forgive as the Lord forgave you."
Colossians 3:13

Forgiveness can be one of the hardest things to do, especially when the hurt runs deep. But Scripture calls us to forgive others as God has forgiven us. Just as we have received His grace, we are to extend that same grace to others. Forgiving doesn't mean condoning the wrong, but it does mean releasing the bitterness and allowing God to heal the hurt. Through forgiveness, we free ourselves from the chains of anger and resentment and open our hearts to God's peace.

Prayer

Lord, help me to forgive those who have hurt me, just as You have forgiven me. Give me the strength to release any bitterness and trust You with my healing.

February 17

Letting Go of Bitterness

"Get rid of all bitterness, rage, and anger, brawling and slander, along with every form of malice. Be kind and compassionate to one another, forgiving each other, just as in Christ God forgave you."

Ephesians 4:31-32

Bitterness can take root in our hearts when we hold onto hurt. It slowly poisons our spirit, keeping us stuck in pain and anger. But God calls us to let go of all bitterness, to choose compassion and forgiveness instead. Letting go doesn't mean pretending the hurt didn't happen, but it means choosing freedom over bondage. As we release bitterness, we make room for God's grace and peace to fill our hearts.

Reflect

Are there areas of your life where bitterness has taken root? Ask God to help you let go of it and fill your heart with His grace and compassion.

February 18

Forgiveness is a Process

"Then Peter came to Jesus and asked, 'Lord, how many times shall I forgive my brother or sister who sins against me? Up to seven times?' Jesus answered, 'I tell you, not seven times, but seventy-seven times.'"

Matthew 18:21-22

Forgiveness is not a one-time act; it's often a process. Sometimes, even after we choose to forgive, the pain resurfaces, and we must forgive again. Jesus taught that forgiveness isn't limited to a certain number of times—it's an ongoing decision to let go of offense and trust God with our wounds. Each time you choose to forgive, you take another step toward healing and freedom. It's okay if it takes time, but don't give up on the process.

Prayer

Lord, I know forgiveness is a journey, and sometimes it feels hard. Help me to walk through this process, trusting You to heal my heart as I continue to forgive.

February 19

Healing Through Forgiveness

"But if you do not forgive others their sins, your Father will not forgive your sins."
Matthew 6:15

Jesus highlights the importance of forgiveness in our own healing. When we hold onto unforgiveness, it creates a barrier between us and God, blocking us from fully experiencing His grace. Forgiveness is not just for the benefit of the person who wronged us; it's for our own spiritual health and healing. When we forgive, we release the hold that pain and anger have on us, and we open ourselves up to the full flow of God's forgiveness and healing in our lives.

Reflect

Is there anyone you need to forgive today? How might holding onto unforgiveness be affecting your relationship with

God?

February 20

Forgiving Yourself

"Therefore, there is now no condemnation for those who are in Christ Jesus."
Romans 8:1

Sometimes the hardest person to forgive is ourselves. We carry guilt, shame, and regret over past mistakes, but God has already forgiven us through Christ. Holding onto self-condemnation only keeps us from fully receiving God's grace. Just as He calls us to forgive others, He also calls us to forgive ourselves. Let go of the guilt you've been holding onto, and allow God's grace to wash over you. You are not condemned—you are forgiven, loved, and free in Christ.

Prayer

Father, I ask for the strength to forgive myself for past mistakes. Help me to see myself through Your eyes—redeemed, loved, and free from condemnation.

February 21

Trusting God with the Outcome

"And we know that in all things God works for the good of those who love Him, who have been called according to His purpose."
Romans 8:28

One of the hardest parts of forgiveness is trusting God with the outcome. We may feel like we're letting someone off the hook, but in reality, we are placing the situation in God's hands. He is the ultimate Judge, and He promises to work all things for our good. When we forgive, we are not excusing the hurt, but we are trusting God to bring justice, healing, and restoration in His way and in His time. Rest in the assurance that God is in control, and He will use even your pain for His purpose.

Reflect

What situations in your life do you need to release into God's hands? How can trusting Him with the outcome bring peace to your heart?

Week 4: Learning to Love Yourself

In our journey of faith, loving ourselves can often be one of the hardest things to do. Yet, it's a vital part of walking in the fullness of God's love. When Jesus calls us to "love your neighbor as yourself," He assumes that we understand and practice self-love, grounded in the truth of who we are in Christ. This week, we'll explore what it means to love ourselves through God's eyes, embrace our identity in Him, and break free from negative thoughts and self-criticism. Loving yourself is not selfish—it is an acknowledgment of the value and worth God has placed in you.

February 22

You Are Fearfully and Wonderfully Made

"I praise You because I am fearfully and wonderfully made; Your works are wonderful, I know that full well."

Psalm 139:14

God created you with intention and purpose. Every part of who you are is known and loved by Him. When we struggle with self-worth or negative self-image, it's easy to forget that we are His masterpiece. Learning to love yourself begins with recognizing that you are fearfully and wonderfully made by a Creator who sees immense value in you. You are not a mistake, and you are not defined by your flaws. God sees you as His beloved creation, unique and precious in His sight.

Reflect

How do you view yourself? Take time to reflect on the truth that you are wonderfully made by God, and let that truth shape how you see yourself.

February 23

Your Identity in Christ

"Therefore, if anyone is in Christ, the new creation has come: The old has gone, the new is here!"
2 Corinthians 5:17

Your identity is not in your past mistakes, your appearance, or what others think of you. In Christ, you are a new creation. The old has passed away, and your worth is found in Him. Embracing your identity in Christ means letting go of the lies and labels the world places on you and instead clinging to the truth that you are a beloved child of God. When you see yourself through God's eyes, you can love yourself with the same grace and compassion that He offers.

Prayer

Lord, help me to embrace my identity in You and to see myself as You see me—redeemed, loved, and made new. Let me find my worth in You alone.

February 24

Breaking Free from Negative Self-Talk

"Finally, brothers and sisters, whatever is true, whatever is noble, whatever is right, whatever is pure, whatever is lovely, whatever is admirable—if anything is excellent or praiseworthy—think about such things."

Philippians 4:8

Negative self-talk can be one of the biggest barriers to loving ourselves. We often speak to ourselves in ways we would never speak to others, filling our minds with harsh criticism and self-doubt. But God calls us to think about what is true, noble, and lovely. Part of loving yourself means speaking words of life and truth over yourself, in alignment with what God says about you. It's about replacing the lies with God's truth, allowing His Word to shape your thoughts and transform your mind.

Reflect

What negative thoughts do you struggle with about yourself? Write down those thoughts, and then counter them with God's truth from His Word.

February 25

Loving Yourself Through Grace

"But He said to me, 'My grace is sufficient for you, for My power is made perfect in weakness.'"

2 Corinthians 12:9

We all have weaknesses and areas where we fall short, but God's grace is more than enough to cover them. Learning to love yourself means giving yourself the same grace that God extends to you. You don't have to be perfect to be loved by God. In fact, it's in your weakness that His power is made perfect.

Instead of being hard on yourself for your shortcomings, embrace the grace God has given you. His grace empowers you to grow, not through striving, but through resting in His love.

Prayer

Lord, help me to extend grace to myself the way You extend it to me. Remind me that Your grace is sufficient, and I am loved in my imperfections.

February 26

Taking Care of Yourself

"Do you not know that your bodies are temples of the Holy Spirit, who is in you, whom you have received from God? You are not your own."

1 Corinthians 6:19

Part of loving yourself is taking care of the body and mind that God has entrusted to you. Your body is a temple of the Holy Spirit, and it's important to honor God by caring for yourself physically, mentally, and emotionally. This includes getting enough rest, nourishing your body with healthy food, exercising, and nurturing your mental and emotional well-being. When we take care of ourselves, we are better able to serve others and fulfill the purpose God has for us.

Reflect

What steps can you take to better care for yourself physically, mentally, and emotionally? Make a plan to prioritize your well-being this week.

February 27

Loving Yourself by Setting Boundaries

"Above all else, guard your heart, for everything you do flows from it."
Proverbs 4:23

Healthy boundaries are essential to loving yourself and guarding your heart. Boundaries protect your emotional, spiritual, and physical well-being. They help you say "no" when needed and prevent you from overextending yourself. Setting boundaries is not selfish—it's an act of self-care that honors the person God has created you to be. When you establish healthy boundaries, you are better able to serve others without losing yourself in the process.

Prayer: Lord, give me the wisdom to set healthy boundaries in my life. Help me to guard my heart and prioritize my well-being, so that I can love and serve others from a place of wholeness.

February 28

Loving Yourself as God Loves You

"We love because He first loved us."
1 John 4:19

Loving yourself begins with receiving God's love. His love is the source of all love, and when we understand how deeply He loves us, it becomes easier to love ourselves. God's love is unconditional, unchanging, and everlasting. He loves you fully, just as you are, and nothing can separate you from that love. When you learn to love yourself as God loves you, you live from a place of security and peace, knowing that you are worthy of love because He says so.

Reflect

How does knowing God's love for you impact how you love yourself? Spend time in prayer, asking God to fill your heart with His love and help you see yourself through His eyes.

3

March

Week 1: Walking by Faith, Not by Sight

Faith is the foundation of our relationship with God. It calls us to trust in what we cannot see, to lean on God's promises, even when circumstances seem uncertain. Walking by faith, not by sight, means we place our trust in God's Word and His character, even when life's challenges make it hard to understand His plan. This week, we will explore what it means to live by faith in our daily lives, trusting God in every step, no matter the circumstances.

March 1

Faith is Confidence in God

"Now faith is confidence in what we hope for and assurance about what we do not see."

Hebrews 11:1

Faith is not just wishful thinking—it's the confident assurance that God's promises will come to pass, even when we can't see how. It's trusting that what God has said is true, regardless of our current reality. We may not have all the answers, and life's uncertainties may test our faith, but we can trust that God is faithful. He will fulfill His promises in His timing, and our job is to walk confidently in that assurance.

Reflect

Are there areas in your life where you are struggling to trust God? Take time to meditate on His promises and ask for His help in building your faith.

March 2

Trusting God's Timing

"For we live by faith, not by sight."

2 Corinthians 5:7

Walking by faith often means surrendering our desire to control outcomes and trusting God's perfect timing. There are moments in life where we want immediate answers, solutions, or relief, but faith asks us to wait on God's timing. He sees the bigger picture and knows what is best for us, even when we don't. Learning to trust God's timing is one of the most challenging but rewarding aspects of walking by faith. He knows what you need and when you need it, so rest in His timing.

Prayer

Lord, help me to trust Your timing, even when I feel anxious or uncertain. Remind me that Your plan is perfect, and I can walk confidently by faith, knowing You are in control.

March 3

Stepping Out in Faith

"The LORD had said to Abram, 'Go from your country, your people and your father's household to the land I will show you.'"

Genesis 12:1

Abram (later Abraham) had no idea where God was leading him, but he obeyed and stepped out in faith. Sometimes God calls us to take steps without revealing the full plan. He asks us to trust Him one step at a time. Faith is not about seeing the entire journey but about being willing to follow where He leads, even into the unknown. Just as Abram trusted God with each step, we too are called to obey God's leading, even when it feels uncertain or scary.

Reflect

Is there a step of faith God is calling you to take? How can you respond in obedience, trusting that He will guide you?

March 4

Faith Overcomes Fear

"So do not fear, for I am with you; do not be dismayed, for I am your God. I will strengthen you and help you; I will uphold you with my righteous right hand."

Isaiah 41:10

Fear is one of the biggest obstacles to walking by faith. When we face challenges, fear often whispers that we are alone or that things will go wrong. But God reminds us repeatedly in Scripture, "Do not fear." He is with us, and He promises to strengthen and uphold us. Faith is trusting that God is greater than our fears. When we choose faith over fear, we acknowledge that God is bigger than any challenge we face, and we walk in confidence, knowing that He is in control.

Prayer

Lord, help me to overcome my fears with faith in You. Remind me that You are with me, guiding and strengthening me in every step I take.

March 5

Faith That Moves Mountains

"Truly I tell you, if you have faith as small as a mustard seed, you can say to this mountain, 'Move from here to there,' and it will move. Nothing will be impossible for you."

Matthew 17:20

Faith doesn't have to be enormous to be powerful. Jesus tells us that even faith as small as a mustard seed can move mountains. What are the mountains in your life? It could be a situation that seems insurmountable, a relationship that feels broken, or a dream that feels out of reach. Whatever it is, remember that God is not limited by our circumstances. When we place our faith in Him, even the smallest amount, He can do the impossible. Trust Him with your mountains, and believe that He can move them in His perfect way.

Reflect

What mountain are you facing right now? Pray for the faith to trust God to move it, knowing that nothing is impossible for Him.

March 6

The Testing of Your Faith

"Consider it pure joy, my brothers and sisters, whenever you face trials of many kinds, because you know that the testing of your

faith produces perseverance."

James 1:2-3

Trials are a part of life, but they serve a purpose in God's plan. The testing of your faith is not meant to break you but to strengthen you and develop perseverance. When we go through difficult times, our faith is refined and made stronger. It's in the valleys of life that we learn to rely on God more deeply and trust Him more fully. While trials may not be joyful in the moment, we can find joy in knowing that God is using them to grow our faith and make us more like Him.

Prayer

Lord, help me to see the trials I face as opportunities for growth. Strengthen my faith through these challenges, and help me to persevere with joy, knowing You are at work in my life.

March 7

Living a Life of Faith

"But my righteous one will live by faith. And I take no pleasure in the one who shrinks back.

Hebrews 10:38

Faith is not just a momentary act—it's a way of life. God calls us to live by faith in everything we do, not shrinking back when challenges arise but trusting Him fully. This means relying on Him in our decisions, seeking His guidance daily, and stepping out in obedience, even when the path is unclear. Living a life of faith is a journey that requires daily surrender and trust in God's promises. As we walk by faith, we grow closer to God and experience the fullness of His plans for our lives.

Reflect

What does living a life of faith look like for you? How can you cultivate a deeper trust in God in your daily walk?

Week 2: Overcoming Doubt

Doubt is a natural part of our spiritual journey. At times, we may struggle to believe God's promises, question our worth, or wonder if we are truly hearing from Him. Yet, God calls us to bring our doubts to Him, trusting that He is greater than our uncertainties. Overcoming doubt doesn't mean we never question; rather, it means we choose to trust God even in the midst of our doubts. This week, we will explore how to confront doubt with faith and how God can use our doubts to deepen our relationship with Him.

March 8

Doubt is Not the Enemy of Faith

"Immediately the boy's father exclaimed, 'I do believe; help me overcome my unbelief!'"
Mark 9:24

The father in Mark's Gospel desperately wanted healing for his son, but he struggled with unbelief. In his honest cry to Jesus, he expressed both faith and doubt. Jesus did not reject him for his doubt; instead, He responded with compassion and healed his son. This shows us that doubt is not the enemy of faith—it's often a sign that we are wrestling with the deep questions of life and faith. God welcomes our doubts, as they can be a pathway to stronger belief when we bring them to

Him honestly.

Reflect

What doubts are you currently facing? How can you bring them to God in prayer, asking Him to help you overcome your unbelief?

March 9

Remembering God's Faithfulness

"I will remember the deeds of the LORD; yes, I will remember Your miracles of long ago."

Psalm 77:11

When doubt creeps in, one of the best ways to combat it is by remembering God's faithfulness in the past. The psalmist reminds us to look back on God's deeds and miracles, allowing those memories to strengthen our faith for the present. God has been faithful before, and He will be faithful again. By recalling the times God has come through for you, or by reading stories of His faithfulness in Scripture, you can remind your heart that He is trustworthy and will fulfill His promises.

Reflect

Take time to write down or reflect on specific moments in your life when God has shown His faithfulness. How can these memories help you overcome your doubts today?

March 10

Trusting God's Character

"God is not human, that He should lie, not a human being, that He should change His mind. Does He speak and then not act? Does He promise and not fulfill?"

Numbers 23:19

When we doubt, it often stems from questioning God's character or His promises. We may wonder, "Will God really come through for me?" Yet, Scripture reassures us that God is not like humans—He does not lie or change His mind. His promises are sure, and His character is unchanging. When we anchor our faith in who God is, rather than in our circumstances or feelings, we find solid ground to stand on. Trusting God's character is key to overcoming doubt.

Prayer

Lord, help me to trust Your unchanging character, especially when my circumstances are uncertain. Remind me that You are faithful and that Your promises never fail.

March 11

Doubt in the Waiting

"Wait for the LORD; be strong and take heart and wait for the LORD."

Psalm 27:14

Waiting on God can often give rise to doubt. When answers don't come quickly, or when we face long seasons of uncertainty, we may wonder if God has forgotten us. But waiting is an important part of the journey of faith. It's in the waiting that God is working behind the scenes, growing our trust and refining our hearts. Instead of letting doubt take over, we can use seasons of waiting to press deeper into God, trusting that His timing is perfect and His plans are good.

Reflect

Are you in a season of waiting? How can you trust God's timing and His plan, even when it's difficult to see what He is doing?

March 12

When Circumstances Challenge Your Faith

"Trust in the LORD with all your heart and lean not on your own understanding; in all your ways submit to Him, and He will make your paths straight."

Proverbs 3:5-6

When life's circumstances don't make sense, it can be easy to lean on our own understanding and let doubt creep in. But God calls us to trust Him with all our heart, even when we can't see the full picture. His ways are higher than our ways, and His understanding is beyond what we can grasp. Trusting God means surrendering our need for control and relying on Him, knowing that He is working all things for our good, even in difficult situations.

Prayer

Lord, help me to trust You completely, especially when my circumstances challenge my faith. Give me peace that surpasses understanding, and help me lean on You instead of my own reasoning.

March 13

Overcoming the Fear of Doubt

"For God has not given us a spirit of fear, but of power and of love and of a sound mind."

2 Timothy 1:7

Sometimes we fear doubt itself, believing that it weakens our faith or separates us from God. But doubt does not have to lead to fear. God has given us a spirit of power, love, and a sound mind to confront our doubts with courage. When we face doubt with honesty and openness before God, it can actually lead to greater intimacy with Him. Don't be afraid of your questions. Instead, trust that God is big enough to handle your doubts and guide you through them with love and wisdom.

Reflect

How can you reframe your doubts, seeing them as an opportunity for growth rather than something to fear? Bring your questions to God and trust Him to provide clarity.

March 14

Faith That Grows Through Doubt

"Blessed is the one who perseveres under trial because, having stood the test, that person will receive the crown of life that the Lord has promised to those who love Him."

James 1:12

Doubt is often part of the testing of our faith. It's not a sign of weak faith but a pathway to deeper trust in God. When we persevere through doubt and seek God in the midst of our questions, our faith grows stronger. God uses these moments to refine our hearts and deepen our reliance on Him. As we come out on the other side of doubt, we experience a more mature faith and a greater understanding of His goodness and faithfulness.

Reflect

How has doubt challenged your faith in the past, and how has God used it to grow you? What steps can you take today to continue seeking God in the midst of your doubts?

Week 3: Boldly Living Out Your Faith

Living out your faith with boldness means more than simply believing in God privately—it means living in a way that openly reflects His love, truth, and grace in every part of your life. It's about stepping into the world confidently as a representative of Christ, standing firm in your beliefs, and sharing the hope you have in Him. This week, we'll explore what it means to be courageous in your faith, letting God's light shine through you in a way that impacts those around you.

March 15

The Power of Boldness in Christ

"The wicked flee though no one pursues, but the righteous are as bold as a lion."

Proverbs 28:1

God calls His people to live with courage and boldness, not in fear or hesitation. When we trust in God, we can stand firm like a lion, bold in the face of challenges, knowing that we are covered by His righteousness. Boldness doesn't come from our strength but from the confidence that God is with us. As believers, we don't have to shrink back in fear or uncertainty. We can live powerfully for Christ, knowing that He empowers us.

Reflect

In what areas of your life do you feel hesitant to live out your faith boldly? Ask God to help you step out in courage and confidence.

March 16

Boldness in Sharing the Gospel

"For I am not ashamed of the gospel, because it is the power of God that brings salvation to everyone who believes."

Romans 1:16

One of the most courageous ways we can live out our faith is by sharing the gospel with others. The world may not always receive it warmly, but as believers, we are called to share the good news of Jesus without shame. The gospel is the power of God for salvation, and by boldly sharing it, we offer others the hope, love, and truth that only Christ can provide. It's not always easy to share our faith, but God equips us to do so with love, wisdom, and boldness.

Prayer

Lord, give me the boldness to share Your gospel with those around me. Help me to speak with love and truth, unashamed of the good news that brings salvation.

March 17

Living with Integrity

"In the same way, let your light shine before others, that they may see your good deeds and glorify your Father in heaven."

Matthew 5:16

Boldly living out your faith means letting your life reflect the character of Christ. One of the most powerful witnesses we can have is through our actions—living with integrity, kindness, and love. When our words and deeds align with our faith, we shine the light of Christ in a way that draws others to Him. This requires boldness because it means standing apart from the world's standards and holding fast to godly principles in every area of life.

Reflect

How can your actions today reflect Christ's love and truth? What steps can you take to live with greater integrity in your daily walk?

March 18

Boldness in Facing Opposition

"Be on your guard; stand firm in the faith; be courageous; be strong."

1 Corinthians 16:13

Living out your faith boldly often means facing opposition, whether from society, relationships, or personal struggles. Standing firm in your faith in the midst of criticism or rejection can be difficult, but God gives us the strength to endure. Bold faith is not about avoiding challenges; it's about trusting God through them. When we stand firm in Christ, even in the face of opposition, we demonstrate that our faith is unshakable.

Prayer

Lord, help me to stand firm in my faith when I face opposition. Give me the courage to remain strong in You, trusting that You will give me the strength to endure.

March 19

Boldly Walking in Obedience

"But Peter and the apostles answered, 'We must obey God rather than men.'"

Acts 5:29

There will be times when living out your faith means choosing obedience to God over pleasing people. Boldness in faith sometimes requires making hard decisions, standing up for what is right, or walking away from situations that compromise your values. Peter and the apostles boldly declared that obedience to God was their highest priority, even when it put them in danger. Likewise, we are called to live in radical obedience to God, no matter the cost, trusting that He will honor our faithfulness.

Reflect

Are there areas in your life where you need to choose obedience to God over pleasing others? How can you take steps to align your life more fully with His will?

March 20

Boldness Through the Holy Spirit

"Now, Lord, consider their threats and enable Your servants to speak Your word with great boldness."

Acts 4:29

True boldness comes from the Holy Spirit. When the early believers prayed for boldness, God responded by filling them with His Spirit and empowering them to preach the Word courageously. We, too, can ask the Holy Spirit for boldness in our daily lives. Whether it's sharing the gospel, making difficult decisions, or standing firm in our beliefs, the Holy Spirit equips us with the courage and power we need. Boldness is not something we muster on our own—it's a gift from God that enables us to live out our faith with confidence.

Prayer

Holy Spirit, fill me with boldness today. Empower me to live for Christ with courage, to speak the truth in love, and to stand firm in my faith.

March 21

The Fruit of Bold Faith

"Therefore, my dear brothers and sisters, stand firm. Let nothing move you. Always give yourselves fully to the work of the Lord, because you know that your labor in the Lord is not in vain."
1 Corinthians 15:58

Boldly living out your faith may not always bring immediate results, but it is never in vain. When we live courageously for Christ, we plant seeds that God will grow in His perfect time. Whether we see the fruit of our boldness today or years from now, we can trust that God is working through our obedience. Bold faith leads to lives transformed by the gospel, and our efforts in the Lord will ultimately bear eternal fruit.

Reflect

How can you give yourself fully to the work of the Lord today? In what areas do you need to continue standing firm, trusting that your labor for God is not in vain?

Week 4: Faith That Moves Mountains

Jesus spoke of a faith so powerful that it could move mountains, symbolizing seemingly impossible situations and challenges. This kind of faith isn't based on the size of our belief but on the greatness of the God we trust. "Mountain-moving faith" is grounded in an unshakable trust in God's power, His promises, and His timing. This week, we will explore what it means to develop this kind of faith—faith that can break through obstacles, overcome trials, and bring about God's miraculous work in our lives.

March 22

The Power of Mustard Seed Faith

"Truly I tell you, if you have faith as small as a mustard seed, you can say to this mountain, 'Move from here to there,' and it will move. Nothing will be impossible for you."
Matthew 17:20

Jesus reminds us that even the smallest amount of genuine faith can accomplish great things. It's not the size of your faith but the object of your faith that matters. When your trust is placed in the all-powerful God, even a mustard seed of faith can move mountains. God is not asking for perfect or enormous faith, but for a heart that believes in His ability to do the impossible.

Reflect

What mountains are you currently facing in your life? Offer them to God, trusting that even your smallest steps of faith can lead to great transformation.

March 23

Faith in God's Timing

"For the vision is yet for an appointed time; it speaks of the end and will not prove false. Though it linger, wait for it; it will certainly come and will not delay."
Habakkuk 2:3

Having mountain-moving faith often involves waiting on God's perfect timing. Sometimes, we may feel like our prayers aren't being answered or that God's promises are delayed, but faith trusts that God is working even when we can't see it. His timing is always perfect, and He will fulfill His promises in the right season. As you wait on God, remember that delays do not mean denials—trust His timing.

Prayer

Lord, give me the patience and trust to wait for Your perfect timing. Help me to believe that You are at work, even when I can't see it yet.

March 24

Overcoming Fear with Faith

"So do not fear, for I am with you; do not be dismayed, for I am your God. I will strengthen you and help you; I will uphold you with My righteous right hand."

Isaiah 41:10

Fear often stands in the way of our faith, making mountains seem immovable. But God repeatedly reminds us in Scripture not to fear because He is with us. When we focus on the size of our problems, fear grows. But when we focus on the size of our God, faith overcomes fear. The mountains in your life may be big, but God is bigger. He promises to strengthen and uphold you as you walk through every challenge.

Reflect

Are there fears holding you back from fully trusting God? Surrender those fears to Him today and ask Him to fill your heart with faith instead.

March 25

Praying Bold, Faith-Filled Prayers

"Therefore I tell you, whatever you ask for in prayer, believe that

you have received it, and it will be yours."
Mark 11:24

Mountain-moving faith is expressed in prayer. Jesus encourages us to pray with boldness and belief, knowing that God hears and responds to our prayers. When we pray with faith, we are aligning our hearts with God's will and trusting that He is able to do far more than we could ever imagine. Bold prayers come from a place of deep trust in God's power and His willingness to act on our behalf.

Prayer

Lord, help me to pray with boldness, trusting that You hear my prayers and are able to do the impossible. Increase my faith to believe in Your miraculous power.

March 26

Faith in the Midst of Trials

"Consider it pure joy, my brothers and sisters, whenever you face trials of many kinds, because you know that the testing of your faith produces perseverance."
James 1:2-3

Trials can feel like mountains blocking our path, but God often uses these challenges to strengthen our faith. It's in the testing of our faith that perseverance and spiritual maturity are developed. Instead of being discouraged by trials, we can see them as opportunities for our faith to grow. The mountains we face are not meant to defeat us but to refine us, shaping us into people who trust God more deeply.

Reflect

How can you see your current challenges as opportunities

for growth in your faith? Ask God to give you the strength and perspective to persevere through them.

March 27

Speaking to Your Mountain

"Jesus replied, 'Have faith in God. Truly I tell you, if anyone says to this mountain, "Go, throw yourself into the sea," and does not doubt in their heart but believes that what they say will happen, it will be done for them.'"

Mark 11:22-23

Jesus teaches us that faith is not passive—it speaks to the mountains in our lives. When we face obstacles, we can boldly declare God's promises over them, trusting that He has the power to move them. Whether it's a situation that seems impossible or a personal struggle that feels overwhelming, we can speak faith-filled words, standing on the truth of God's Word and believing that He will act.

Reflect

What mountains do you need to speak to in faith? Spend time declaring God's promises over those situations, trusting Him to move powerfully.

March 28

Faith That Perseveres

"Let us hold unswervingly to the hope we profess, for He who promised is faithful."

Hebrews 10:23

Mountain-moving faith requires perseverance. There will be times when you don't see immediate results, but faith holds on to hope, trusting in the faithfulness of God. We are called to stand firm in our belief that God is able, even when the mountain hasn't yet moved. Persevering in faith means continuing to trust God's goodness and power, even in the waiting and through the challenges. God honors faith that endures.

Prayer

Lord, help me to hold on to faith even when the mountain doesn't move right away. Give me the strength to persevere, knowing that You are always faithful to Your promises.

March 29

Faith Rooted in God's Promises

"Let us hold unswervingly to the hope we profess, for He who promised is faithful."
Hebrews 10:23

Persevering faith holds tight to God's promises, trusting that He is faithful. Even when circumstances seem uncertain, we can cling to His Word and find hope. Knowing God's promises strengthens us, reminding us that He will never leave us or forsake us. Today, choose a promise from Scripture and meditate on it, letting it anchor your faith in God's unchanging character.

Reflection

Which promise of God resonates with you today? How can it help you persevere in faith through any challenges you are facing?

Prayer

Lord, thank You for Your promises that remind me of Your faithfulness. Help me to hold firmly to them, trusting You even when life feels uncertain. Strengthen my faith to persevere, knowing that You will always be true to Your Word.

March 30

Confidence in Christ

Scripture: "So we can confidently say, 'The Lord is my helper; I will not fear; what can man do to me?'"
Hebrews 13:6

Living boldly in faith doesn't mean we never feel afraid or uncertain. It means that we choose to trust in God's power over any fear or challenge that may come our way. The world offers countless reasons to doubt, worry, or question, but with God as our helper, we have every reason to stand firm. Confidence in Christ is about recognizing that our identity, worth, and strength come from Him alone. When our lives are rooted in this confidence, our faith becomes a testimony to others.

Prayer

Lord, help me to root my confidence in You, knowing that You are my strength and helper. When I feel uncertain, remind me of Your unwavering presence. May my life reflect Your power and peace. Amen.

March 31

Being a Light

Scripture: "You are the light of the world. A town built on a hill cannot be hidden." Matthew 5:14

Living out your faith boldly means allowing the light of Christ within you to shine for others to see. Faith isn't something to keep hidden; it's meant to be shared openly and joyfully. Think about how your words, actions, and choices can point others toward God. Being a light in the world doesn't require perfection—it simply means living authentically, loving openly, and showing grace even in difficult situations. When we let our light shine, we become beacons of hope, peace, and love in a world that so desperately needs them.

Prayer

Jesus, You are the light of my life. Help me to live in a way that brings Your love and truth to others. Teach me to be a beacon of Your grace and compassion, sharing Your light wherever I go. Amen.

4

April

Week 1: Embracing God's Grace

God's grace is one of the most beautiful and transformative gifts we can ever receive. It's His unmerited favor, extended to us not because of anything we've done, but because of who He is. Embracing God's grace means understanding that His love, forgiveness, and acceptance are freely given, and that His grace empowers us to live in freedom, joy, and purpose. This week, we'll explore what it means to fully embrace God's grace, allowing it to shape our identity, heal our brokenness, and guide us into a deeper relationship with Him.

April 1

What Is God's Grace?

"For it is by grace you have been saved, through faith—and this is not from yourselves, it is the gift of God."

Ephesians 2:8

God's grace is His gift to us—a gift we could never earn or deserve. It is through His grace that we are saved and brought into a relationship with Him. His grace is not something we can work for or achieve by our own efforts, but it is given freely because of His love for us. Understanding grace is foundational to our faith, and it changes the way we see God, ourselves, and others.

Reflect

How does understanding grace as a gift from God change the way you view your relationship with Him? Take time to thank God for His grace and meditate on how it has impacted your life.

April 2

Grace That Covers Our Failures

"But He said to me, 'My grace is sufficient for you, for My power is made perfect in weakness.'"
2 Corinthians 12:9

God's grace doesn't just save us—it sustains us through every weakness, failure, and struggle. His grace is more than enough to cover our mistakes and shortcomings. Often, we feel we need to have everything together before coming to God, but grace reminds us that His power shines through our weaknesses. We don't need to be perfect for God to love us; His grace is sufficient, and His strength is made perfect when we admit our need for Him.

Prayer

Lord, thank You that Your grace is sufficient for me. Help me to rest in Your grace and rely on Your strength, especially in areas where I feel weak or inadequate.

April 3

Living in the Freedom of Grace

"It is for freedom that Christ has set us free. Stand firm, then, and do not let yourselves be burdened again by a yoke of slavery."
Galatians 5:1

Grace brings freedom. When we embrace God's grace, we are freed from the burden of trying to earn His love or live up to impossible standards. We are no longer slaves to fear, guilt, or the pressure to perform. Instead, we are invited to live in the freedom that comes from knowing we are fully accepted by God. Grace allows us to rest in the knowledge that we are loved just as we are, while also empowering us to live transformed lives.

Reflect

Are there areas of your life where you feel like you have to "earn" God's love or approval? Ask God to help you fully embrace the freedom of His grace.

April 4

Grace in Our Relationships

"Be kind and compassionate to one another, forgiving each other, just as in Christ God forgave you."
Ephesians 4:32

When we receive God's grace, it transforms the way we relate to others. Just as God has shown us undeserved kindness, patience, and forgiveness, we are called to extend that same grace to those around us. This can be challenging, especially when others hurt us or let us down, but God's grace empowers us to forgive and love others, even when it's difficult. Grace reminds us that we have all fallen short, and yet we are all recipients of God's love and mercy.

Prayer

Lord, help me to extend the same grace to others that You have shown to me. Teach me to forgive quickly, love unconditionally, and show kindness to those around me.

April 5

Grace for Every Season

"Let us then approach God's throne of grace with confidence, so that we may receive mercy and find grace to help us in our time of need."

Hebrews 4:16

God's grace is available to us in every season of life, whether we are walking through joy or hardship. We can come confidently before God, knowing that He offers grace to help us in our time of need. His grace sustains us through the challenges we face, giving us strength, wisdom, and peace. No matter what you are going through, God's grace is sufficient, and He invites you to approach Him boldly to receive all that you need.

Reflect

In what areas of your life do you need to rely more on God's grace? Bring those areas to Him in prayer and trust that He will provide the grace you need.

April 6

Grace That Transforms

"For the grace of God has appeared that offers salvation to all people. It teaches us to say 'No' to ungodliness and worldly

passions, and to live self-controlled, upright, and godly lives in this present age."
Titus 2:11-12

God's grace not only forgives our sins but also transforms our hearts and lives. It empowers us to live in a way that honors God. Grace is not a license to continue in sin, but it is the power to live a new life in Christ. As we grow in our understanding of God's grace, it teaches us to turn away from the things that pull us away from God and to embrace a life of righteousness, love, and holiness.

Prayer

Father, thank You that Your grace not only saves me but also transforms me. Help me to live in a way that reflects Your grace and to grow in holiness as I follow You.

April 7

Growing in Grace

"But grow in the grace and knowledge of our Lord and Savior Jesus Christ. To Him be glory both now and forever! Amen."
2 Peter 3:18

Embracing God's grace is not a one-time event but a lifelong journey. We are called to continually grow in grace, allowing it to shape every area of our lives. This means daily choosing to live in the freedom, forgiveness, and love that God has given us, and also allowing His grace to overflow into our relationships and interactions with others. As we grow in grace, we grow in our relationship with God, becoming more like Christ and reflecting His grace to the world.

Reflect

How can you continue to grow in grace this week? Ask God to help you deepen your understanding of His grace and live it out in every area of your life.

Week 2: Showing Grace to Others

As recipients of God's boundless grace, we are called to extend that same grace to those around us. Showing grace means offering forgiveness, patience, and love even when it's undeserved, just as God has done for us. This week, we will dive into the practical and spiritual aspects of extending grace to others, learning how to reflect God's character in our relationships, and how showing grace can transform both our hearts and the lives of those around us.

April 8

Grace Freely Given, Grace Freely Given Away

"Freely you have received; freely give."

Matthew 10:8

God's grace is a gift we receive, not something we earn. Just as we have been freely forgiven and loved by God, we are called to offer the same grace to others. Sometimes, it's hard to extend grace to those who have hurt us or let us down, but remembering how freely God has given grace to us helps us to pass it on. When we give grace, we become instruments of God's love and mercy in the lives of others.

Reflect

Think of someone in your life who may need to experience grace through you. How can you extend God's grace to them today, even if it's difficult?

April 9

Forgiving as Christ Forgave

"Bear with each other and forgive one another if any of you has a grievance against someone. Forgive as the Lord forgave you."
Colossians 3:13

Forgiveness is one of the most powerful ways we show grace to others. It's also one of the hardest. Holding on to anger, resentment, or bitterness can block us from experiencing the fullness of God's grace in our own lives. Jesus calls us to forgive just as He has forgiven us, which means letting go of offenses, no matter how deep they run. When we forgive, we are freed from the chains of unforgiveness and can walk in peace and freedom.

Prayer

Lord, help me to forgive others as You have forgiven me. Heal my heart from any wounds and give me the strength to extend grace to those who have hurt me.

April 10

The Power of Grace in Our Words

"Do not let any unwholesome talk come out of your mouths, but only what is helpful for building others up according to their needs, that it may benefit those who listen."
Ephesians 4:29

Our words have the power to either build up or tear down. One way we can show grace to others is through the words we speak. Speaking with kindness, gentleness, and encouragement can bring life and healing to those around us. When we choose grace-filled words, we reflect the heart of God, who speaks truth and love over us. This doesn't mean avoiding hard conversations, but approaching them with compassion and grace.

Reflect

Are your words reflecting God's grace in your relationships? Take a moment to consider how you can be more intentional about speaking words that build others up.

April 11

Showing Patience and Kindness

"Love is patient, love is kind. It does not envy, it does not boast, it is not proud."

1 Corinthians 13:4

Patience and kindness are expressions of grace in our everyday interactions. When people frustrate or disappoint us, our natural reaction might be to respond in anger or impatience. But grace calls us to respond with patience and kindness, even when it's hard. In showing patience, we demonstrate God's enduring love for us, and in showing kindness, we reflect His heart of compassion.

Prayer

Father, give me the strength to respond with patience and kindness, even in difficult situations. Help me to reflect Your love in the way I treat others.

April 12

Choosing Grace in Conflict

"If it is possible, as far as it depends on you, live at peace with

everyone."
Romans 12:18

Conflict is an inevitable part of life, but grace offers a way to handle it with wisdom and love. Instead of seeking revenge or harboring bitterness, we are called to pursue peace. Grace doesn't mean avoiding difficult conversations or pretending problems don't exist, but it does mean choosing to approach conflict with humility, seeking understanding and reconciliation. When we allow grace to lead us in conflict, we can turn moments of tension into opportunities for growth and healing.

Reflect

Is there a relationship in your life where conflict has taken root? How can you bring grace into that situation, seeking peace and reconciliation?

April 13

Grace for Those Who Are Hard to Love

"But love your enemies, do good to them, and lend to them without expecting to get anything back. Then your reward will be great, and you will be children of the Most High, because He is kind to the ungrateful and wicked."
Luke 6:35

It's easy to show grace to those who are kind to us, but Jesus challenges us to go further—extending grace to those who are difficult to love. Whether it's someone who has hurt us, a difficult coworker, or even someone who opposes us, grace calls us to love unconditionally. Loving our enemies, doing good to those who wrong us, and expecting nothing in return is a reflection of God's grace, which He offers even to those who reject Him.

Prayer

Lord, help me to show grace to those who are hard to love. Give me a heart that reflects Your unconditional love, even toward my enemies.

April 14

Grace as a Way of Life

"Let your conversation be always full of grace, seasoned with salt, so that you may know how to answer everyone."
Colossians 4:6

Living a life full of grace means making grace a daily practice, not just an occasional choice. Grace should flow through our words, actions, and attitudes, coloring the way we interact with others. When grace becomes a way of life, we become people who reflect God's love in every situation, offering forgiveness, kindness, and patience wherever we go. Living this way allows us to share the transformative power of God's grace with a world in need.

Reflect

How can you make grace a more consistent part of your daily life? Ask God to help you live in such a way that His grace shines through you in every interaction.

Week 3: Grace in Difficult Circumstances

Life's challenges and hardships can sometimes make it difficult to feel or extend grace. Yet, it is precisely in these tough times that God's grace can shine the brightest. Grace in difficult circumstances is about relying on God's strength when we feel weak, trusting His plan when we don't understand, and showing grace to others even when life is hard. This week, we will explore how God's grace can carry us through our toughest moments, offering peace, strength, and hope when we need it most.

April 15

God's Grace Is Sufficient in Weakness

"But He said to me, 'My grace is sufficient for you, for My power is made perfect in weakness.'"

2 Corinthians 12:9

When we are faced with difficult circumstances, we often feel weak, inadequate, or overwhelmed. Yet, God's response to our weakness is grace—His power is made perfect in our moments of deepest need. We don't have to rely on our own strength to get through challenges; instead, we can lean on God's grace, which is more than enough. His grace not only sustains us but empowers us to endure and even grow stronger in difficult seasons.

Reflect

In what areas of your life are you feeling weak or overwhelmed? How can you invite God's grace into those areas and trust Him to sustain you?

April 16

Trusting God's Grace When Life Doesn't Make Sense

"And we know that in all things God works for the good of those who love Him, who have been called according to His purpose."

Romans 8:28

There are times in life when things don't make sense—when we face loss, disappointment, or unexpected challenges. It's easy to wonder where God is in the midst of our pain. However, God's grace reminds us that He is always at work, even in the hardest circumstances. Though we may not understand His plan, we can trust that He is weaving everything together for our good. His grace gives us the ability to trust Him, even when we don't have all the answers.

Prayer

Lord, help me to trust Your grace in the midst of uncertainty. Even when I don't understand what You're doing, I choose to believe that You are working all things together for my good.

April 17

Grace That Brings Peace in Storms

"Peace I leave with you; My peace I give you. I do not give to you as the world gives. Do not let your hearts be troubled and do not be afraid."

John 14:27

God's grace brings peace that transcends our circumstances. Even in the middle of life's storms, His peace is available to calm our anxious hearts. The world's peace depends on external conditions, but the peace that comes from God is rooted in His presence and His promises. No matter what storms you are facing, His grace offers you peace that can guard your heart and mind, reminding you that He is with you through it all.

Reflect

Are you struggling with anxiety or fear in your current circumstances? Take time to surrender your worries to God and ask for His peace to fill your heart.

April 18

Grace for Perseverance

"Let us not become weary in doing good, for at the proper time we will reap a harvest if we do not give up."
Galatians 6:9

When challenges persist and difficulties seem to drag on, it's easy to grow weary. Yet God's grace gives us the perseverance we need to keep going, even when the road is long and hard. His grace sustains us when we feel like giving up and strengthens us to continue trusting Him and doing what is right, knowing that in time, we will see the fruit of our faithfulness.

Prayer

Lord, give me the grace to persevere through the challenges I am facing. Help me to remain steadfast and to trust that You are working in my situation, even when I can't see it.

April 19

Grace in the Face of Loss

"The Lord is close to the brokenhearted and saves those who are crushed in spirit."
Psalm 34:18

Loss, whether it's the loss of a loved one, a job, a dream, or something we deeply value, can be one of the most painful experiences we go through. In moments of loss, God's grace offers comfort and healing. He draws near to the brokenhearted and offers His presence as a source of peace and strength. Grace doesn't always remove the pain of loss, but it assures us that we are not alone and that God is with us in our grief, carrying us through it.

Reflect

Are you going through a season of loss? Allow yourself to grieve, but also invite God's grace to comfort and heal your heart. Trust that He is near, even in your sorrow.

April 20

Grace to Respond with Love

"But I tell you, love your enemies and pray for those who persecute you."

Matthew 5:44

When we face difficult people or unfair treatment, our natural response is often anger, bitterness, or a desire for revenge. But God's grace calls us to respond in a radically different way—with love, even toward those who hurt us. Showing grace in difficult relationships is one of the most challenging yet transformative ways we can reflect God's character. It doesn't mean ignoring wrongs or allowing ourselves to be mistreated, but it does mean choosing to respond with forgiveness, kindness, and love, trusting that God will handle the rest.

Prayer

Lord, help me to show grace to those who have wronged me. Give me the strength to respond with love and forgiveness, even when it's hard.

April 21

Strengthened by Grace

"You then, my son, be strong in the grace that is in Christ Jesus."
2 Timothy 2:1

Grace is not only something we receive but also something that strengthens us. When we face trials, we can draw strength from the grace that is ours in Christ. His grace equips us to endure hardships, empowers us to overcome obstacles, and gives us the courage to face whatever comes our way. No matter how tough the circumstances, God's grace is available to give us the strength we need to stand firm in our faith and continue walking in His purpose.

Reflect

Where do you need God's strength in your life right now? Ask Him to fill you with His grace and give you the strength to persevere through whatever challenges you are facing.

Week 4: Grace for Yourself

Sometimes the hardest person to extend grace to is ourselves. We can be quick to offer forgiveness and understanding to others, but we often hold ourselves to impossible standards, burdened by guilt, shame, or a constant need for perfection. This week, we will focus on learning to accept God's grace for ourselves. We will explore how to let go of self-condemnation, embrace God's forgiveness, and walk in the freedom that comes from receiving His grace in our own lives.

April 22

Accepting God's Forgiveness

"If we confess our sins, He is faithful and just and will forgive us our sins and purify us from all unrighteousness."

1 John 1:9

One of the first steps to offering grace to yourself is accepting God's forgiveness. Often, we hold on to guilt and shame long after God has forgiven us, believing we need to "make up" for our mistakes. But God's grace is not something we earn—it's freely given. When we confess our sins, God is faithful to forgive, and He no longer holds our mistakes against us. It's time to release yourself from the guilt and accept the complete forgiveness that God has offered.

Reflect

Are you holding on to guilt or shame for something God has already forgiven? Take time today to confess and receive His grace, knowing that He has fully forgiven you.

April 23

Letting Go of Perfectionism

"But He said to me, 'My grace is sufficient for you, for My power is made perfect in weakness.'"

2 Corinthians 12:9

Perfectionism is the enemy of grace. When we try to be perfect, we end up striving in our own strength, constantly feeling like we're not enough. But God's grace is sufficient even in our weaknesses. He doesn't ask us to be perfect—He asks us to rely on Him. By letting go of perfectionism, we make room for God's grace to fill our imperfections. His power is made perfect in our weakness, and His grace allows us to walk in freedom instead of striving.

Prayer

Lord, help me to let go of the need to be perfect. Remind me that Your grace is enough, and that I don't have to strive for perfection to be loved and accepted by You.

April 24

Overcoming Self-Condemnation

"Therefore, there is now no condemnation for those who are in Christ Jesus."

Romans 8:1

Self-condemnation is a heavy burden to carry. We can be our own worst critics, constantly replaying our failures and mistakes. Yet, God's grace frees us from the weight of condemnation. In Christ, we are no longer condemned—our past sins, mistakes, and failures have been wiped clean. It's time to silence the voice of self-condemnation and embrace the truth of God's grace, which declares that we are forgiven, loved, and free.

Reflect

Are you carrying the weight of self-condemnation? Take a moment to release those burdens to God and remind yourself that in Christ, there is no condemnation.

April 25

Learning to Rest in Grace

"Come to Me, all you who are weary and burdened, and I will give you rest."

Matthew 11:28

Life can feel overwhelming, especially when we constantly feel the need to "do better" or "be more." But God invites us to rest in His grace. Instead of striving to meet impossible expectations or burning ourselves out trying to achieve more, we can rest in the fact that God's grace is enough. Resting in grace means trusting that God's love for us isn't based on our performance, but on His goodness. It allows us to stop striving and to find peace in His presence.

Prayer

Lord, help me to rest in Your grace. When I feel overwhelmed by life's demands or my own expectations, remind me that Your grace is enough, and I can find rest in You.

April 26

Giving Yourself Grace in Failure

"For though the righteous fall seven times, they rise again."
Proverbs 24:16

Failure is a part of life, and how we respond to it matters. God's grace gives us the freedom to fail without fear of rejection. When we fall, His grace lifts us back up and gives us the strength to keep moving forward. Instead of beating ourselves up for every mistake, we can learn to give ourselves grace, trusting that God's love and acceptance don't change when we fail. His grace empowers us to rise again, stronger and more reliant on Him.

Reflect

How do you typically respond to failure? Today, ask God to help you extend grace to yourself in the areas where you've fallen short, knowing that His grace is greater than your failures.

April 27

Embracing Who God Made You to Be

"For we are God's handiwork, created in Christ Jesus to do good works, which God prepared in advance for us to do."
Ephesians 2:10

God's grace extends to who we are, not just what we do. Sometimes, we struggle with accepting ourselves—our personality, our gifts, or even our physical appearance. But God created you intentionally, with purpose and love. Embracing who God made you to be means accepting His grace over your life, celebrating the unique way He has formed you, and trusting that He has good plans for you. God's grace covers every part of who you are, and He delights in you.

Prayer

Lord, help me to embrace who You created me to be. Teach me to see myself through Your eyes, filled with grace and love, and to celebrate the unique person You have made me.

April 28

Walking in Freedom and Grace

"It is for freedom that Christ has set us free. Stand firm, then, and do not let yourselves be burdened again by a yoke of slavery."
Galatians 5:1

God's grace sets us free—not just from sin, but from the burdens of self-condemnation, perfectionism, and shame. Walking in grace means walking in the freedom Christ has already won for us. We are no longer bound by the need to prove ourselves or live up to impossible standards. Instead, we can live in the freedom of being fully loved, fully accepted, and fully forgiven. As you walk in grace, let go of the things that weigh you down and embrace the freedom that comes from living in God's grace.

Reflect

Are there areas of your life where you still feel burdened or trapped by unrealistic expectations or guilt? Ask God to help you walk in the freedom of His grace, letting go of those burdens and embracing the abundant life He has for you.

5

May

Week 1: Choosing Joy

Joy is not always a natural response to life's circumstances, but it is a fruit of the Spirit that we are invited to choose every day. It isn't dependent on external situations but comes from a deep well of faith in God's goodness. This week, we will focus on what it means to choose joy in every season, whether in abundance or difficulty. We'll explore how God's presence, promises, and purpose fill our hearts with joy, regardless of what life brings.

May 1

The Source of Our Joy

"The joy of the Lord is your strength."
Nehemiah 8:10

True joy comes from God. It isn't based on how we feel or what is happening around us but is rooted in who God is and what He has done for us. The joy of the Lord strengthens us, giving us the ability to endure and persevere, even when life is hard. When we anchor our joy in God, we find that nothing in this world can take it away. His joy becomes our strength, sustaining us through every circumstance.

Reflect

What is currently stealing your joy? How can you refocus your heart on the joy that comes from God, rather than on your circumstances?

May 2

Joy in God's Presence

"You make known to me the path of life; You will fill me with joy in Your presence, with eternal pleasures at Your right hand."

Psalm 16:11

God's presence is a source of joy. When we spend time with Him—whether in prayer, worship, or reading His Word—He fills our hearts with joy that surpasses anything this world can offer. In His presence, we find peace, comfort, and delight. Choosing joy means choosing to seek God's presence, even when life feels heavy or uncertain. As we draw near to Him, His joy overflows into our hearts, giving us the strength to face whatever comes our way.

Prayer

Lord, fill my heart with joy as I spend time in Your presence. Help me to seek You each day and to find my delight in knowing You.

May 3

Joy in Trials

"Consider it pure joy, my brothers and sisters, whenever you face trials of many kinds, because you know that the testing of your faith produces perseverance."
James 1:2-3

Joy in trials may seem counterintuitive, but Scripture teaches us that trials can produce perseverance and spiritual maturity. When we face difficult times, we can choose joy—not because the trial is easy, but because we trust that God is using it for our good. He is refining our faith, strengthening our character, and drawing us closer to Him. Choosing joy in trials means believing that God is in control and that He is working all things together for our growth and His glory.

Reflect

Are you going through a difficult season? How can you choose to find joy in the knowledge that God is using this time to strengthen your faith and draw you closer to Him?

May 4

Finding Joy in Gratitude

"Give thanks in all circumstances; for this is God's will for you in Christ Jesus."
1 Thessalonians 5:18

Gratitude is closely connected to joy. When we cultivate a heart of thankfulness, even in difficult circumstances, we open ourselves up to experience deeper joy. Giving thanks helps us focus on God's goodness and provision, reminding us that He is always at work in our lives. No matter what we are facing, there is always something to be thankful for. As we practice gratitude, we shift our focus from what we lack to what we have, allowing joy to flourish in our hearts.

Prayer

Lord, help me to cultivate a heart of gratitude. Even in hard times, show me the blessings You have placed in my life, and teach me to give thanks in all circumstances.

May 5

Joy in Serving Others

"I have told you this so that My joy may be in you and that your joy may be complete."

John 15:11

One of the ways we experience God's joy is through serving others. Jesus came to serve, and as we follow His example, we find that our joy becomes complete. When we shift our focus from ourselves to the needs of others, we experience the joy of being used by God to bless and encourage. Serving others with love and kindness not only brings joy to them but also fills our hearts with a deep sense of fulfillment and purpose.

Reflect

How can you serve someone today? Ask God to show you ways to bless others and experience the joy that comes from living with a servant's heart.

May 6

Joy in God's Promises

"May the God of hope fill you with all joy and peace as you trust in Him, so that you may overflow with hope by the power of the Holy Spirit."

Romans 15:13

God's promises are a source of unshakable joy. When we place our hope in His Word and trust in His faithfulness, joy overflows in our hearts. His promises remind us that no matter what we face, He is with us, He is for us, and He has good plans for our lives. Choosing joy means holding on to His promises, even when our circumstances are uncertain, and allowing His Word to fill us with hope, peace, and joy.

Prayer

Lord, help me to trust in Your promises. Fill my heart with joy and peace as I put my hope in You, knowing that You are faithful to fulfill all that You have promised.

May 7

Joy in Surrendering to God's Will

"Delight yourself in the Lord, and He will give you the desires of your heart."

Psalm 37:4

Surrendering to God's will doesn't mean giving up joy—it means finding deeper joy in His perfect plan for our lives. When we delight in Him and trust His will, we find that He fills our hearts with joy that aligns with His desires for us. Surrendering to God allows us to experience the freedom and joy that comes from knowing He is in control and that His plans are far greater than anything we could imagine. True joy is found not in getting our way, but in aligning our hearts with His.

Reflect

Is there an area of your life that you need to surrender to God? Ask Him to help you trust His plan and find joy in His will for your life.

Week 2: Finding Joy in Trials

Finding joy in the midst of trials can seem like a difficult task. Trials often bring pain, uncertainty, and frustration, but God invites us to look beyond our circumstances and discover joy in Him, even in hardship. This week, we will explore how to view trials through the lens of faith, trusting that God is working through every difficulty to produce growth, strength, and deeper reliance on Him.

May 8

Joy Through Endurance

"Consider it pure joy, my brothers and sisters, whenever you face trials of many kinds, because you know that the testing of your faith produces perseverance."

James 1:2-3

James teaches us to consider trials as an opportunity for joy because they develop perseverance. Trials are not meaningless; they strengthen our faith and help us grow in spiritual maturity. Endurance is built through resistance, and every trial we face is a chance to grow stronger in our walk with God. Choosing joy in trials doesn't mean ignoring pain but embracing the growth God is producing in us through our perseverance.

Reflect

How can you see your current trials as an opportunity for spiritual growth? Ask God to give you the strength to endure and to develop joy through the process.

May 9

Trusting God's Purpose in Pain

"And we know that in all things God works for the good of those who love Him, who have been called according to His purpose."
Romans 8:28

God promises to work all things for our good, including the trials we face. While we may not understand why we are going through difficult times, we can trust that God is using every experience to shape us and draw us closer to Him. Finding joy in trials requires trusting that God has a purpose, even in pain. He is not distant or indifferent to our suffering; He is actively working to bring about good from even the hardest circumstances.

Prayer

Lord, help me trust that You are working all things for my good, even when I don't understand. Teach me to find joy in knowing that You have a purpose for every trial I face.

May 10

Joy in God's Refining Process

"These [trials] have come so that the proven genuineness of your faith—of greater worth than gold, which perishes even though refined by fire—may result in praise, glory, and honor when Jesus Christ is revealed."
1 Peter 1:7

Trials refine our faith like gold refined in fire. Just as gold is purified through intense heat, our faith is purified through the trials we endure. This refining process reveals the strength and genuineness of our faith, preparing us for greater things and deepening our relationship with God. Finding joy in trials means recognizing that God is shaping us into the image of

Christ, using every difficulty to refine and strengthen us for His purposes.

Reflect

How is God refining your faith through the challenges you're facing? Consider the ways He is shaping you, and find joy in the knowledge that you are being made stronger through His refining process.

May 11

Joy in God's Presence During Trials

"The Lord is close to the brokenhearted and saves those who are crushed in spirit."

Psalm 34:18

One of the greatest sources of joy during trials is the assurance that God is near. He doesn't leave us to face difficulties alone; He is close to the brokenhearted and offers His comfort, peace, and strength. Finding joy in trials means leaning on God's presence, trusting that He is walking with us every step of the way. His closeness is a source of deep joy, knowing that we are never alone in our suffering.

Prayer

Lord, thank You for Your presence in my life. Help me to feel Your nearness in the midst of my trials and find joy in the comfort and strength You provide.

May 12

Learning to Rejoice in Suffering

"Not only so, but we also glory in our sufferings, because we know that suffering produces perseverance; perseverance, character; and character, hope."

Romans 5:3-4

Suffering is never easy, but it is a path that leads to hope. The apostle Paul teaches us that suffering produces perseverance, which builds character, and ultimately leads to hope. Joy in trials comes from understanding this transformative process. Every trial is an opportunity for growth, and as our character is strengthened, our hope in God becomes unshakable. Rejoicing in suffering means embracing the long-term benefits of God's work in our hearts, even when the present is painful.

Reflect

How has God used past trials to strengthen your character and build your hope? Reflect on the ways He has worked through suffering in your life, and trust that He is continuing that process now.

May 13

Joy in God's Strength

"The righteous cry out, and the Lord hears them; He delivers them from all their troubles."

Psalm 34:17

Trials can be overwhelming, but we don't have to rely on our own strength to endure them. God promises to hear our cries and deliver us from our troubles. In our weakness, He is our strength, and we can find joy in knowing that He is our refuge. When we feel weary or overwhelmed by life's challenges, we can turn to God for the strength we need to press on. Joy comes from knowing that we don't have to face trials alone—God is our deliverer.

Prayer

Lord, I need Your strength. I feel weary from the trials I am facing, but I trust in Your promise to deliver me. Fill my heart with joy as I lean on Your strength, knowing You are my refuge.

May 14

Joy in God's Faithfulness

"I remain confident of this: I will see the goodness of the Lord in the land of the living."

Psalm 27:13

Even in the darkest times, we can hold on to the promise of God's faithfulness. We may not always see His goodness immediately, but we can trust that He will come through. Finding joy in trials means holding on to hope and knowing that God's goodness will be revealed in His perfect time. He is faithful to His promises, and we can find joy in the confidence that we will experience His goodness again, even in the land of the living.

Reflect

Are you struggling to see God's goodness in your current situation? Take time to remind yourself of His past faithfulness and hold on to the hope that His goodness will come again.

Week 3: Joy in Service

Serving others is one of the most profound ways to experience joy. Jesus Himself modeled a life of service, showing us that true joy comes from loving and giving to others. This week, we will explore how serving others not only blesses them but also fills our hearts with a deep, lasting joy that aligns with God's purpose for our lives. As we pour ourselves out in service, we discover that God fills us up with His joy.

May 15

Following Jesus' Example

"For even the Son of Man did not come to be served, but to serve, and to give His life as a ransom for many."
Mark 10:45

Jesus came not to be served, but to serve. His life was the ultimate example of humility, sacrifice, and love. When we serve others, we follow in His footsteps and reflect His heart to the world. Service requires selflessness and a focus on others, but in doing so, we experience the joy of living like Christ. As we serve, we participate in His mission, and our hearts are filled with the joy that comes from living out our faith in action.

Reflect

How can you follow Jesus' example of service in your everyday life? Think of one way you can serve someone today, and ask God to give you the heart of a servant.

May 16

The Blessing of Giving

"In everything I did, I showed you that by this kind of hard work we must help the weak, remembering the words the Lord Jesus Himself said: 'It is more blessed to give than to receive.'" Acts 20:35

There is a unique joy that comes from giving, whether it's our time, resources, or energy. Jesus taught that it is more blessed to give than to receive, and when we give to others, we open our hearts to the joy that God promises. The blessing of giving is not only in what we offer but also in what God does in us through the act of generosity. Serving others reminds us that we are part of something bigger than ourselves, and it allows us to experience the joy of being a blessing.

Prayer

Lord, teach me the joy of giving. Help me to live generously, knowing that when I give, I am blessed and can bring Your love to those around me.

May 17

Joy in Serving with a Willing Heart

"Serve the Lord with gladness; come before His presence with singing."

Psalm 100:2

Serving is not just about the actions we take but the heart with which we do them. God desires that we serve Him and others with a willing and joyful heart. When we serve out of love for God and a desire to bless others, we find joy in the process. Even mundane or difficult tasks become opportunities to worship and glorify God when our hearts are aligned with His. Serving with gladness transforms our perspective, allowing us to find joy in every act of service.

Reflect

Do you approach service with a joyful and willing heart? Consider how you can shift your perspective to serve others with gladness, knowing that you are serving God in the process.

May 18

Finding Joy in Small Acts of Kindness

"And if anyone gives even a cup of cold water to one of these little ones who is My disciple, truly I tell you, that person will certainly not lose their reward."

Matthew 10:42

Sometimes, we think that service has to be grand or significant to matter, but Jesus reminds us that even the smallest acts of kindness are valuable in God's eyes. Whether it's offering a kind word, a helping hand, or a simple act of generosity, every gesture of service is important. Joy comes from knowing that God sees and values every act of love we offer to others, no matter how small. Serving others in little ways can make a big impact, both in their lives and in ours.

Prayer

Lord, help me to see the opportunities for small acts of kindness today. Let me find joy in serving others in simple, everyday ways, knowing that even the smallest service brings You glory.

May 19

Joy in Using Your Gifts for Others

"Each of you should use whatever gift you have received to serve others, as faithful stewards of God's grace in its various forms."

1 Peter 4:10

God has given each of us unique gifts and talents, not just for our own benefit, but to serve others. When we use our gifts to bless others, we experience the joy of fulfilling God's purpose for our lives. Serving with the gifts God has entrusted to us brings a deep sense of satisfaction and joy because we are doing what we were created to do. Whether your gift is teaching, encouraging, helping, or leading, God's grace flows through you when you serve others with the gifts He has given you.

Reflect

What gifts has God given you that you can use to serve others? Consider how you can steward these gifts to bless those around you and experience the joy of living out your calling.

May 20

Joy in Serving Without Recognition

"But when you give to the needy, do not let your left hand know what your right hand is doing, so that your giving may be in secret. Then your Father, who sees what is done in secret, will reward you."
Matthew 6:3-4

True joy in service comes when we don't seek recognition or praise. Jesus teaches us to serve in humility, without the need for acknowledgment from others. God sees every act of service, even when no one else does, and He rewards us in ways far greater than human applause. Serving quietly and humbly allows us to focus on the needs of others and the joy of pleasing God, rather than seeking approval or validation from those around us.

Prayer

Lord, help me to serve with a humble heart. Let my service be for Your glory, not for my own recognition, and remind me that You see every act of love, no matter how small.

May 21

Joy in Eternal Impact

"Therefore, my dear brothers and sisters, stand firm. Let nothing move you. Always give yourselves fully to the work of the Lord, because you know that your labor in the Lord is not in vain."
1 Corinthians 15:58

One of the greatest sources of joy in service is knowing that what we do for the Lord has eternal value. Our service may not always be easy or glamorous, but it has a lasting impact in the kingdom of God. When we give ourselves fully to God's work, we can trust that our labor is never in vain. Every act of service, no matter how small, contributes to God's greater plan and purpose. Joy comes from the assurance that our service matters in God's eternal kingdom.

Reflect

How can you remind yourself that your service has eternal significance? Reflect on the ways God is using you to impact others, and find joy in knowing that your labor for the Lord will bear fruit, even if you can't see it yet.

Week 4: Joy in God's Presence

There is no greater source of joy than being in the presence of God. His presence brings peace, fulfillment, and a deep sense of belonging. This week, we will reflect on how to experience the fullness of joy that comes from abiding in God's presence, recognizing that His nearness is not dependent on our circumstances, but is always available to us. Through prayer, worship, and quiet moments with Him, we can discover the richness of joy that flows from our connection with the Creator.

May 22

Fullness of Joy in His Presence

"You make known to me the path of life; in Your presence there is fullness of joy; at Your right hand are pleasures forevermore."

Psalm 16:11

God's presence is the ultimate source of joy, a joy that is complete and overflowing. In His presence, we find not just fleeting happiness but a deep and abiding joy that satisfies our souls. When we turn our hearts toward Him and seek to dwell in His presence, we experience the fullness of life as He intended it. This joy transcends circumstances because it is rooted in who God is, not in what is happening around us.

Reflect

How can you intentionally seek God's presence today? Spend time in prayer or worship, inviting God to fill you with the fullness of His joy.

May 23

The Joy of Abiding in Him

"As the Father has loved Me, so have I loved you. Now remain in My love. If you keep My commands, you will remain in My love, just as I have kept My Father's commands and remain in His love. I have told you this so that My joy may be in you and that your joy may be complete."

John 15:9-11

Abiding in Christ means staying connected to Him, remaining in His love, and following His commands. When we live in close relationship with Jesus, we experience the joy that comes from being in alignment with God's will. Jesus promised that

His joy would be in us, and our joy would be made complete when we remain in Him. This joy is a result of living in constant communion with Him, drawing on His strength and love in every aspect of life.

Prayer

Lord, help me to remain in You, abiding in Your love and following Your ways. May Your joy fill my heart as I stay connected to You each day.

May 24

Joy in Worship

"Come, let us sing for joy to the Lord; let us shout aloud to the Rock of our salvation. Let us come before Him with thanksgiving and extol Him with music and song."

Psalm 95:1-2

Worship is a powerful way to experience the joy of God's presence. When we come before Him with songs of praise, thanksgiving, and adoration, we align our hearts with His, and His joy fills us. Worship shifts our focus from our problems to His greatness, reminding us of His goodness and faithfulness. Whether in a corporate setting or in personal times of worship, we encounter God's presence in a unique way, and His joy floods our souls.

Reflect

Take time today to worship God through music, singing, or simply thanking Him for who He is. Allow His presence to fill you with joy as you praise Him.

May 25

Joy in Quiet Moments with God

"Be still, and know that I am God."
Psalm 46:10a

In the busyness of life, we often forget the joy that can be found in simply being still before God. Quiet moments with Him allow us to hear His voice, experience His peace, and rest in His presence. In these moments, we are reminded that God is in control, and we don't have to strive to experience His joy. Instead, we can simply be still, knowing that He is with us, and let His joy fill our hearts in the calmness of His presence.

Prayer

Lord, help me to find joy in the quiet moments with You. As I quiet my heart and mind, let me sense Your presence and rest in the joy that comes from being still before You.

May 26

Joy in His Unfailing Love

"But I trust in Your unfailing love; my heart rejoices in Your salvation."
Psalm 13:5

God's love for us is unfailing, and in His love, we find a reason to rejoice, even in difficult times. His love never changes, never diminishes, and never fails. When we reflect on the depth of God's love, we are reminded of how secure we are in Him, and this security brings joy. No matter what we face, we can rejoice in the salvation He has given us and the steadfastness of His love. His presence is a constant source of joy because His love never wavers.

Reflect

Reflect on God's unfailing love for you today. How does

knowing that He loves you unconditionally bring you joy? Rejoice in the security of His love and salvation.

May 27

Joy in Knowing God Is Near

"The Lord is near to all who call on Him, to all who call on Him in truth."

Psalm 145:18

God is never far from us; He is always near and ready to respond when we call on Him. Knowing that God is close brings great comfort and joy, especially in times of need. When we call on Him in prayer, we are reminded of His presence and His readiness to hear us. The nearness of God gives us peace and fills our hearts with joy, because we know we are never alone, no matter what we face.

Prayer

Lord, thank You for being near to me. Help me to call on You in every situation, trusting that You are always with me. Let Your presence fill me with joy as I walk with You daily.

May 28

Joy in His Eternal Presence

"You have made known to me the path of life; You will fill me with joy in Your presence, with eternal pleasures at Your right hand."

Psalm 16:11

The joy we experience in God's presence on earth is just a glimpse of the eternal joy we will have in His presence forever. In His presence, we are filled with life and joy that never ends. This promise of eternal joy gives us hope and strengthens us in our journey of faith. We can look forward to the day when we will dwell with God forever, where joy will be complete, and sorrow and pain will be no more.

Reflect

How does the promise of eternal joy in God's presence give you hope and strength for today? Rejoice in the assurance that one day, you will be with Him forever, where His joy will never end.

6

June

Week 1: God's Peace in Troubling Times

In a world filled with uncertainty, fear, and hardship, God offers us peace that surpasses all understanding. This week, we will explore how to experience and hold on to God's peace, even in the midst of troubling times. His peace is not dependent on external circumstances but is rooted in His presence, His promises, and His faithfulness. As we lean into Him, we can rest in the calm assurance that He is in control, and His peace will guard our hearts and minds.

June 1

The Gift of Peace

"Peace I leave with you; My peace I give you. I do not give to you as the world gives. Do not let your hearts be troubled and do not be afraid."

John 14:27

Jesus offers us a kind of peace that the world cannot provide—peace that is steady, enduring, and unaffected by circumstances. This peace is a gift from Him, given freely to those who trust in Him. We don't have to earn it or work for it; it's ours to receive. When we accept this peace, it calms our fears and quiets our anxieties, reminding us that God is with us no matter what we face.

Reflect

How can you open your heart to receive the peace that Jesus offers? Take time today to meditate on the fact that His peace is a gift, freely given to you.

June 2

Peace Beyond Understanding

"And the peace of God, which transcends all understanding, will guard your hearts and your minds in Christ Jesus."
Philippians 4:7

God's peace goes beyond what our minds can comprehend. It's a supernatural calm that can exist even in the middle of chaos or uncertainty. This peace doesn't come from everything being perfect but from knowing that God is in control. When we turn to Him in prayer and surrender our worries, His peace stands guard over our hearts and minds, protecting us from fear and anxiety.

Prayer

Lord, I surrender my worries to You today. Fill my heart and mind with Your peace that surpasses understanding. Guard me from fear, and help me trust in Your care.

June 3

Trusting God in the Storm

"Then He got up and rebuked the winds and the waves, and it was completely calm."
Matthew 8:26

When the disciples found themselves in a storm, they panicked, but Jesus was right there with them. With a word, He calmed the wind and the waves. In the storms of life, we often feel overwhelmed, but God is with us in every moment. His presence brings calm, and His power is greater than any storm we face. Even when the storm doesn't immediately end, we can trust that He is in control, and His peace is available to us.

Reflect

What storms are you facing right now? Take a moment to invite Jesus into those situations and ask Him to calm your heart, even if the storm around you hasn't yet subsided.

June 4

Casting Your Anxieties on Him

"Cast all your anxiety on Him because He cares for you."
1 Peter 5:7

God invites us to bring all of our anxieties and concerns to Him. He doesn't want us to carry the weight of worry on our own. When we cast our cares on Him, we acknowledge that He is more than able to handle them. His care for us is personal and tender, and He wants to replace our anxieties with His peace. Trusting Him with our burdens is an act of faith that frees us from the heavy load of worry.

Prayer

Lord, help me to cast my anxieties on You today. I trust

in Your care and Your ability to handle everything that is weighing on my heart. Let Your peace replace my worries.

June 5

Finding Rest in God's Promises

"In peace I will lie down and sleep, for You alone, Lord, make me dwell in safety."

Psalm 4:8

God's promises are a source of peace and rest for our souls. When we rest in His promises, we can lay down our fears and find peace, knowing that He is watching over us. God's promise to be our protector, provider, and guide gives us confidence to face each day without fear. No matter what challenges come our way, His promises are unshakable, and they bring peace to our hearts.

Reflect

What promises of God can you hold onto today that will bring you peace? Spend time reflecting on His promises and trusting that He will fulfill them in your life.

June 6

Peace Through Prayer

"Do not be anxious about anything, but in every situation, by prayer and petition, with thanksgiving, present your requests to God."

Philippians 4:6

Prayer is a powerful way to experience God's peace. When we bring our concerns to Him, we are invited to release our worries and trust in His ability to work in our situations.

Prayer shifts our focus from the problem to the One who holds the solution. Through prayer, we can experience peace, knowing that we are not alone in our struggles and that God is actively at work in our lives.

Prayer

Lord, thank You that I can come to You in prayer and find peace. Help me to bring all of my concerns to You, trusting that You hear me and are working on my behalf.

June 7

Peace in the Presence of the Shepherd

"Even though I walk through the darkest valley, I will fear no evil, for You are with me; Your rod and Your staff, they comfort me."
Psalm 23:4

Even in life's darkest moments, God's presence brings comfort and peace. The Good Shepherd walks with us through every valley, guiding us, protecting us, and providing for us. We don't have to fear because He is near. His presence brings peace that nothing in this world can take away. No matter how deep the valley, His peace sustains us, and His love never leaves us.

Reflect

How does knowing that God is with you in every situation bring you peace? Take comfort in the fact that the Shepherd is guiding you, even through difficult times.

Week 2: Fearlessness Through Faith

Fear can be one of the greatest barriers to living fully in God's promises. It can hold us back from stepping into our purpose and trusting God in difficult situations. However, God calls us to walk in faith, not fear. This week, we will explore how faith in God's power, promises, and presence enables us to live fearlessly. As we trust Him, we discover that fear loses its grip, and we are empowered to walk in boldness, courage, and confidence.

June 8

God Has Not Given You a Spirit of Fear

"For God has not given us a spirit of fear, but of power and of love and of a sound mind."
2 Timothy 1:7

Fear is not from God. He has given us His Spirit, which equips us with power, love, and sound judgment. When fear tries to creep into our minds, we must remember that it is not of God. His Spirit within us gives us the strength to overcome fear and face life's challenges with a heart full of faith. God has empowered us to live boldly, filled with His courage and love.

Reflect

In what areas of your life have you allowed fear to take control? Ask God to replace that fear with the boldness of His Spirit.

June 9

Faith Over Fear

"When I am afraid, I put my trust in You."
Psalm 56:3

Fear is a natural human response to uncertainty and danger, but faith is the spiritual response. When fear arises, we are called to turn our eyes to God and place our trust in Him. Faith doesn't mean we never feel afraid, but it means that when fear comes, we choose to trust God more than we trust our fears. Faith overcomes fear by focusing on God's power and goodness, believing that He is greater than anything we face.

Prayer

Lord, help me to trust You more than I trust my fears. Strengthen my faith so that I can walk boldly, knowing You are in control.

June 10

Courage in the Face of Uncertainty

"Have I not commanded you? Be strong and courageous. Do not be afraid; do not be discouraged, for the Lord your God will be with you wherever you go."
Joshua 1:9

When God called Joshua to lead the Israelites into the Promised Land, He knew Joshua would face overwhelming challenges. Yet, God repeatedly reminded Joshua to be strong and courageous, not because the journey would be easy, but because God would be with him. The same is true for us. When we face uncertainty, we can take heart in knowing that God is with us, guiding and strengthening us. His presence gives us the courage to move forward, even when the path is unclear.

Reflect

What uncertainties are you facing right now? How does knowing that God is with you bring courage and strength?

June 11

Fear Not, for God Is With You

"So do not fear, for I am with you; do not be dismayed, for I am your God. I will strengthen you and help you; I will uphold you with My righteous right hand."
Isaiah 41:10

God's presence is the ultimate antidote to fear. His promise to be with us means that we are never alone in our struggles. When fear threatens to overwhelm us, we can hold on to the assurance that God is right beside us, giving us strength, guidance, and comfort. He upholds us with His righteous right hand, meaning we are safe and secure in His care. We can face anything with confidence when we know that God is with us.

Prayer

Lord, thank You for Your constant presence in my life. Help me to trust in Your strength and refuse to let fear control my heart.

June 12

Faith That Conquers Fear

"The Lord is my light and my salvation—whom shall I fear? The Lord is the stronghold of my life—of whom shall I be afraid?"
Psalm 27:1

When we truly understand who God is, fear loses its power. God is our light, our salvation, and our stronghold. He is our protector and defender. With Him by our side, there is no enemy, situation, or obstacle that we should fear. Faith in God gives us the confidence to stand firm, knowing that He is greater than anything we might face. As we grow in our understanding of His character, our faith grows, and fear diminishes.

Reflect

In what ways can you remind yourself of who God is when fear tries to creep in? Spend time today focusing on God's power and goodness.

June 13

Walking in Boldness

"The wicked flee though no one pursues, but the righteous are as bold as a lion."
Proverbs 28:1

Boldness comes from knowing that we are right with God and that He is on our side. This boldness is not arrogance, but a quiet confidence in God's power and protection. The righteous, those who trust in the Lord, can walk through life with the courage and boldness of a lion, unafraid of what lies ahead. This kind of boldness is a fruit of faith—faith in the truth that God goes before us and stands with us in every situation.

Prayer

Lord, grant me the boldness that comes from knowing I am secure in You. Help me to walk fearlessly in faith, trusting in Your strength and guidance.

June 14

Fearlessness Through God's Love

"There is no fear in love. But perfect love drives out fear, because fear has to do with punishment. The one who fears is not made perfect in love."

1 John 4:18

God's perfect love casts out all fear. When we are fully rooted in His love, we can live fearlessly, knowing that we are completely loved, accepted, and secure in Him. Fear often comes from the unknown or from feelings of inadequacy, but God's love reassures us that He is for us, not against us. His love removes the fear of failure, rejection, or judgment. Living in the truth of His love sets us free to live boldly and courageously.

Reflect

How can God's love drive out fear in your life? Take time to reflect on His deep and perfect love for you, and let it fill your heart with courage.

Week 3: Casting Your Cares on Him

Life can often feel overwhelming, and we all face moments where the weight of worry, anxiety, or burdens seem too much to bear. Yet, God invites us to release our cares and place them in His hands. This week, we will focus on learning how to trust God with our burdens, knowing that He cares deeply for us. As we cast our cares on Him, we'll discover the freedom, peace, and rest that comes from trusting Him with everything we hold onto.

June 15

God Cares for You

"Cast all your anxiety on Him because He cares for you."
1 Peter 5:7

The first step in casting your cares on God is knowing that He genuinely cares for you. God is not distant or indifferent to your struggles. He sees, He knows, and He cares deeply about the burdens you carry. His love for you is tender and personal. When you bring your anxieties to Him, you are not bothering Him—you are coming to the One who is eager to help and comfort you. Trusting in His care allows you to release the weight of your worries into His capable hands.

Reflect

What anxieties have you been holding onto? Take time today to cast those worries on God, trusting in His deep care for you.

June 16

The Invitation to Rest

"Come to Me, all you who are weary and burdened, and I will give you rest."
Matthew 11:28

Jesus extends an open invitation to all who are weary and burdened: come to Him, and He will give you rest. We are not meant to carry the weight of life's stresses and pressures on our own. Jesus invites us to exchange our burdens for His rest. This rest isn't just physical, but a deep, soul-level peace that comes from trusting in His care and provision. As we come to Him with our burdens, He offers us rest for our hearts and minds.

Prayer

Lord, I come to You with my burdens today. Help me to release them into Your hands and rest in Your peace.

June 17

Trusting God with the Unknown

"Trust in the Lord with all your heart and lean not on your own understanding; in all your ways submit to Him, and He will make your paths straight."

Proverbs 3:5-6

One of the greatest sources of anxiety is the fear of the unknown. When we can't see how things will work out, it's easy to become overwhelmed with worry. But God calls us to trust Him completely, even when we don't understand the situation. Trusting God with the unknown means leaning on His wisdom, not our own, and believing that He is working things out for our good. As we trust Him, we can let go of the need to figure everything out ourselves and rest in His perfect plan.

Reflect

What situations in your life are uncertain or unclear? Ask God to help you trust Him fully, even when you don't know what the future holds.

June 18

Surrendering Your Burdens

"Take My yoke upon you and learn from Me, for I am gentle and humble in heart, and you will find rest for your souls. For My yoke is easy and My burden is light."

Matthew 11:29-30

Surrendering your burdens to God is an act of faith and trust. Jesus offers us a lighter burden—His yoke, which is easy and light. When we carry the weight of our worries, we often find ourselves exhausted and discouraged. But when we surrender those burdens to Jesus, He shares the load with us, guiding us in His grace. His gentle care and humility show us that we don't have to carry everything on our own. He is ready to lighten our load and walk with us through life's challenges.

Prayer

Lord, I surrender my burdens to You today. Teach me to walk in Your rest and to trust in Your strength, not my own.

June 19

Releasing Control

"Do not be anxious about anything, but in every situation, by prayer and petition, with thanksgiving, present your requests to God."

Philippians 4:6

Anxiety often stems from a desire to control things that are beyond our ability to manage. We worry because we feel helpless or uncertain about the outcome. But God calls us to release control and bring everything to Him in prayer. Instead of holding onto our worries, we are invited to present our requests to God with thanksgiving, trusting that He hears us and is working on our behalf. When we release control to Him, we find peace in knowing that He is fully capable of handling every situation.

Reflect

What are you trying to control in your life that needs to be released to God? Pray today, asking God to take control and bring you peace in that area.

June 20

Freedom from Worry

"Who of you by worrying can add a single hour to your life?"
Matthew 6:27

Worry accomplishes nothing but adds unnecessary weight to our lives. It cannot change the past or control the future. Jesus reminds us that worrying doesn't add anything to our lives; in fact, it takes away our peace and joy. God knows our needs, and He is fully able to provide for us. Worrying about tomorrow robs us of the peace that God offers today. As we learn to cast our cares on Him, we experience the freedom that comes from trusting Him completely.

Prayer

Lord, help me to release my worries and trust in Your provision. Free me from the weight of worry, and fill my heart with peace.

June 21

God's Peace Guards Your Heart

"And the peace of God, which transcends all understanding, will guard your hearts and your minds in Christ Jesus."
Philippians 4:7

When we cast our cares on God, His peace fills our hearts and minds. This peace is not dependent on our circumstances but is rooted in His presence and His promises. God's peace transcends all human understanding—it doesn't always make sense, but it is real and powerful. As we release our worries to Him in prayer, He promises to guard our hearts and minds with His peace. This peace protects us from fear, anxiety, and doubt, allowing us to rest in His care.

Reflect

How has God's peace guarded your heart in the past? Spend time today thanking Him for His peace and asking Him to fill your heart with it once again.

Week 4: Renewing Your Confidence in God

There are seasons in life when our confidence in God can waver—when we face setbacks, disappointments, or prolonged difficulties. Yet, God calls us to continually renew our trust and confidence in Him. This week, we will explore what it means to live with a renewed sense of trust in God's faithfulness and His ability to work all things for our good. Through His Word, we can rediscover the strength and courage that come from placing our confidence fully in Him.

June 22

Confidence in God's Promises

"Let us hold unswervingly to the hope we profess, for He who promised is faithful."
Hebrews 10:23

God's promises are a firm foundation for our confidence. He is always faithful to fulfill His Word, even when we can't see how things will unfold. When life feels uncertain or overwhelming, it's important to remind ourselves of what God has promised. His Word is full of assurances that He will never leave us, will provide for us, and will guide us through every trial. Holding onto His promises allows us to live with unshakable confidence, knowing that God will be true to His Word.

Reflect

What promises of God can you cling to today? Take time to meditate on His faithfulness and how He has kept His Word in your life.

June 23

Trusting God's Timing

"The Lord is good to those who hope in Him, to the one who seeks Him; it is good to wait quietly for the salvation of the Lord."
Lamentations 3:25-26

One of the hardest aspects of faith is trusting God's timing. We often want things to happen on our schedule, but God knows the perfect time for everything. Learning to wait on Him, without growing impatient or discouraged, is key to renewing our confidence in His plan. As we wait, we can trust that He is working behind the scenes, orchestrating circumstances for our good. In the waiting, God builds our character, strengthens our faith, and prepares us for the blessings to come.

Prayer

Lord, help me to trust Your timing and wait patiently for You. Strengthen my faith as I trust in Your perfect plan for my life.

June 24

Overcoming Doubt

"But when you ask, you must believe and not doubt, because the one

who doubts is like a wave of the sea, blown and tossed by the wind."
James 1:6

Doubt can creep in when we experience setbacks or when things don't go as planned. Yet, God calls us to stand firm in our faith, trusting that He is able to do what He has promised. Overcoming doubt requires us to remind ourselves of who God is and what He has done in the past. When we focus on His power, His goodness, and His faithfulness, our confidence in Him is renewed. We are no longer tossed by the winds of doubt but are anchored in His unchanging truth.

Reflect

In what areas of your life have you allowed doubt to take hold? Ask God to strengthen your faith and renew your confidence in His ability to provide.

June 25

Courage in the Face of Challenges

"So we say with confidence, 'The Lord is my helper; I will not be afraid. What can mere mortals do to me?'"
Hebrews 13:6

Life's challenges can sometimes cause us to lose heart, but God gives us courage when we place our confidence in Him. Knowing that He is our helper, protector, and provider, we can face any obstacle with boldness. Fear and doubt lose their power when we remind ourselves that God is on our side. As we renew our confidence in God, we find the courage to stand firm in the face of adversity, trusting that He will see us through.

Prayer

Lord, help me to find courage in You today. Strengthen my heart and renew my confidence in Your power to help me overcome the challenges I face.

June 26

Confidence in God's Provision

"And my God will meet all your needs according to the riches of His glory in Christ Jesus."

Philippians 4:19

God promises to provide for all of our needs, and we can have confidence that He will take care of us. His provision isn't limited to material needs; He also provides emotional, spiritual, and relational support. When we trust in His provision, we are freed from the worry of how things will work out. God knows exactly what we need and when we need it, and He is faithful to supply all of our needs out of His abundant resources.

Reflect

Are there areas of your life where you are struggling to trust God's provision? Pray for renewed confidence in His ability to meet your needs.

June 27

Finding Strength in God's Presence

"The Lord is my strength and my shield; my heart trusts in Him, and He helps me. My heart leaps for joy, and with my song I praise Him."

Psalm 28:7

Confidence in God grows when we rest in His presence. He is our source of strength, our shield in times of trouble. As we draw near to Him, we experience the joy and peace that comes from being in His presence. His strength renews us, and His help sustains us through life's trials. When we feel weak or uncertain, we can trust that God's presence is enough to carry us through. Renewing our confidence in Him means resting in the truth that He is always with us, ready to help and strengthen us.

Prayer

Lord, I find my strength in You today. Renew my confidence in Your presence, and remind me that You are always near, ready to help.

June 28

Unshakable Confidence in God's Love

"And so we know and rely on the love God has for us. God is love. Whoever lives in love lives in God, and God in them."

1 John 4:16

At the core of our confidence in God is the knowledge of His unchanging love for us. When we know that we are loved by God, we can face anything with confidence. His love casts out fear, strengthens our faith, and gives us hope. Renewing your confidence in God often starts with remembering His deep love for you. No matter what challenges or doubts you face, you can trust that His love is constant and unfailing. In His love, we are secure and unshakable.

Reflect

How can you rely on God's love more deeply in your life? Spend time today meditating on the truth that you are fully and completely loved by God.

7

July

Week 1: Worship as a Lifestyle

Worship is often thought of as something we do on Sunday mornings or during special services, but it is so much more than that. Worship is a way of life, a response to the greatness of God that shapes our thoughts, actions, and relationships. This week, we will explore what it means to live a lifestyle of worship, recognizing that every moment can be an opportunity to honor and glorify God. Through our daily choices, attitudes, and actions, we can express our love for Him and align our lives with His purpose.

July 1

Understanding True Worship

"Yet a time is coming and has now come when the true worshipers will worship the Father in the Spirit and in truth, for they are the kind of worshipers the Father seeks."

John 4:23

True worship is not confined to a specific place or time; it is about connecting with God from the heart. Jesus teaches us that God seeks worshipers who come to Him in Spirit and truth. This means that our worship should be sincere, reflecting our genuine love and adoration for Him. As we begin this week, take time to reflect on what true worship looks like in your life. How can you cultivate a deeper, more authentic relationship with God through your worship?

Reflect

What does it mean to you to worship in Spirit and truth? Consider how you can express this in your daily life.

July 2

Worship in Everyday Moments

"So whether you eat or drink or whatever you do, do it all for the glory of God."

1 Corinthians 10:31

Worship is not limited to singing or praying; it encompasses every aspect of our lives. In 1 Corinthians, Paul reminds us that even the mundane acts of eating and drinking can be done as an act of worship when we do them for the glory of God. This perspective shifts how we view our daily tasks, turning routine moments into opportunities to honor Him. As we cultivate a lifestyle of worship, we can seek to glorify God in our actions, words, and attitudes throughout the day.

Prayer

Lord, help me to see every moment as an opportunity to worship You. Teach me how to glorify You in my everyday activities.

July 3

The Power of Praise

"I will praise the Lord at all times; His praise will always be on my lips."

Psalm 34:1

Praise is a vital aspect of worship that transforms our hearts and minds. When we choose to praise God, regardless of our circumstances, we shift our focus from our problems to His greatness. This act of worship invites His presence into our lives and helps us recognize His goodness. As we cultivate a habit of praise, we will find joy, strength, and encouragement in even the most challenging situations. This week, make it a priority to express your praise to God, both in good times and in bad.

Reflect

How can you incorporate more praise into your daily routine? Consider starting or ending each day by expressing gratitude and adoration to God.

July 4

Worship Through Service

"Whatever you do, work heartily, as for the Lord and not for men."

Colossians 3:23

Worship is not just about what we say; it's also about how we serve. Serving others is a profound expression of our love for God and our commitment to His purposes. When we serve with a heart of worship, we honor God by reflecting His love and compassion to those around us. This can take many forms—volunteering, helping a neighbor, or simply offering a kind word. By viewing our service as an act of worship, we bring glory to God and demonstrate our faith in action.

Prayer

Lord, help me to see my service to others as an act of worship. Show me ways I can serve those around me to reflect Your love.

July 5

The Role of Community in Worship

"Let us consider how we may spur one another on toward love and good deeds, not giving up meeting together, as some are in the habit of doing, but encouraging one another."

Hebrews 10:24-25

Worship thrives in community. God designed us to be in relationship with one another, encouraging and uplifting each other in our faith. Gathering together as a community provides opportunities for collective worship, sharing testimonies, and supporting one another. When we come together, we can spur one another on toward love and good deeds, reminding each other of God's faithfulness. Embrace the importance of community in your worship journey, and seek ways to be involved in the lives of those around you.

Reflect

How can you encourage and uplift others in your faith community? Consider reaching out to someone this week to share encouragement or support.

July 6

Worship Through Obedience

"If you love me, keep my commands."

John 14:15

Our obedience to God is a significant form of worship. When we align our lives with His will and follow His commands, we demonstrate our love and trust in Him. Worship is not only about our expressions of love but also about living out that love through our actions. By choosing to obey God, we reflect His character and bring glory to His name. This week, focus on areas of your life where you can express your love for God through obedience.

Prayer

Lord, help me to demonstrate my love for You through my obedience. Show me areas where I can align my actions with Your will.

July 7

A Life Transformed by Worship

"Therefore, I urge you, brothers and sisters, in view of God's mercy, to offer your bodies as a living sacrifice, holy and pleasing to God—this is your true and proper worship."

Romans 12:1

Living a lifestyle of worship means offering every part of our lives to God. Paul calls us to present ourselves as living sacrifices, which requires us to surrender our desires and ambitions in exchange for His will. This kind of worship transforms us from the inside out, aligning our hearts with God's purpose. As we commit to living for Him in every aspect of our lives, we will experience the joy and fulfillment that comes from being in a right relationship with our Creator.

Reflect

What does it look like for you to be a living sacrifice for God? Spend time today considering how you can offer every part of your life as an act of worship.

Week 2: Worship in the Hard Times

Life is filled with challenges, and there are moments when our circumstances can feel overwhelming. During these difficult times, worship may be the last thing on our minds. However, it is often in our struggles that we can experience the deepest connection with God. This week, we will explore how worship can be a powerful response to hardship, drawing us closer to God and reminding us of His faithfulness, even in our darkest hours.

July 8

Acknowledging Our Pain

"The Lord is close to the brokenhearted and saves those who are crushed in spirit."

Psalm 34:18

Worship begins with honesty. In difficult times, it's essential to acknowledge our pain and struggles rather than pretend everything is okay. God invites us to bring our burdens to Him, to lay our hearts bare, and to express our sorrow. When we approach Him with our brokenness, we can experience His nearness and comfort. Recognizing our pain is the first step toward healing and allows us to turn our focus to the One who can help us through.

Reflect

What burdens are you carrying today? Take a moment to express your pain to God, knowing that He is close to you in your struggle.

July 9

Worship as an Act of Faith

"Though He slay me, yet will I hope in Him; I will surely defend my ways to His face."

Job 13:15

In the story of Job, we see a man who faced unimaginable loss and suffering yet chose to worship God despite his circumstances. Worshiping during hard times is an act of faith, a declaration that we trust God's character even when we don't understand His plans. It can be a powerful way to reaffirm our hope in Him. This week, consider how you can express your faith through worship, even when your heart feels heavy.

Prayer

Lord, help me to worship You, even when I don't understand what is happening in my life. Strengthen my faith to trust You through the storms.

July 10

Finding Strength in Worship

"But those who hope in the Lord will renew their strength. They will soar on wings like eagles; they will run and not grow weary, they will walk and not be faint."

Isaiah 40:31

Worship can be a source of strength during difficult times.

When we turn our hearts toward God in worship, we invite His presence into our struggles, allowing Him to renew our strength and give us hope. It can shift our focus from our problems to His greatness. As we worship, we can find peace, reassurance, and the ability to carry on, knowing that God is with us and will sustain us through our trials.

Reflect

How has worship provided strength in your life? Consider setting aside time this week to engage in worship—through music, prayer, or reading Scripture—to renew your strength in Him.

July 11

The Role of Community in Worshiping Through Trials

"Carry each other's burdens, and in this way you will fulfill the law of Christ."

Galatians 6:2

In hard times, we often need the support of our faith community. Worshiping together can be a powerful source of encouragement and strength. When we share our burdens with one another, we remind each other of God's faithfulness and love. This week, reach out to your community—whether it's through a church group, friends, or family—and let them know how they can pray for you or support you during this time. Join together in worship, even if it's just a simple prayer or sharing a song that uplifts your spirits.

Prayer

Lord, thank You for the community of believers around me. Help me to lean on them and to support others as we walk through difficult times together.

July 12

Worship as a Weapon Against Fear

"For God has not given us a spirit of fear, but of power, love, and a sound mind."

2 Timothy 1:7

Fear can often accompany hardship, threatening to overwhelm us and cloud our judgment. However, worship can serve as a powerful weapon against fear. When we focus on God's character—His love, power, and faithfulness—we are reminded that we do not face our struggles alone. Worship helps to realign our perspective, allowing us to rise above our fears and rest in the peace that only God can provide. This week, take time to actively engage in worship as a way to combat fear in your life.

Reflect

What fears are you facing right now? Write them down and counter each one with a truth about God's character or a promise from Scripture.

July 13

Grieving and Worshiping Simultaneously

"Jesus wept."

John 11:35

Worshiping in hard times doesn't mean we have to suppress our grief or pretend we are not hurting. Jesus Himself experienced deep sorrow, and in John 11:35, we see His humanity displayed as He weeps over the death of His friend Lazarus. Our worship can coexist with our grief; both are valid responses to life's challenges. Allow yourself to grieve while also bringing your heart before God in worship. This week, reflect on how you can embrace both emotions and honor God through your process of healing.

Prayer

Lord, help me to grieve openly and honestly while also seeking You in my pain. Teach me how to worship You in the midst of my sorrow.

July 14

Hope for the Future Through Worship

"For I know the plans I have for you," declares the Lord, "plans to prosper you and not to harm you, plans to give you hope and a future."

Jeremiah 29:11

Worshiping in hard times is an act of hope. It reminds us that God has a plan for our lives, even when we cannot see it. As we reflect on His goodness and faithfulness, we can find comfort in the truth that He will ultimately bring about good in our lives. Worship anchors us in this hope and empowers us to keep moving forward. This week, spend time in worship as a declaration of your trust in God's future for you, knowing that He is always working behind the scenes for your good.

Reflect

What hopes do you have for the future? Spend time in prayer and worship, laying those hopes before God and trusting in His plans for your life.

Week 3: The Power of Praise

Praise is a vital aspect of our relationship with God, serving as a powerful tool for expressing our love, gratitude, and faith. When we praise God, we align our hearts with His truth and declare His greatness over our lives and circumstances. This week, we will explore the transformative power of praise and how it can impact our spiritual lives, strengthen our faith, and deepen our connection with God.

July 15

The Call to Praise

"Let everything that has breath praise the Lord. Praise the Lord!"
Psalm 150:6

The Bible calls us to praise God in every circumstance, reminding us that praise is a fundamental expression of our faith. Praising God is not limited to certain moments but should be a continuous aspect of our lives. When we intentionally choose to praise Him, we shift our focus from our problems to His goodness and faithfulness. This week, reflect on the many reasons you have to praise God, regardless of your circumstances.

Reflect

Take a moment to list things you are grateful for today. How can you express your gratitude to God through praise?

July 16

The Transformative Nature of Praise

"You turned my wailing into dancing; you removed my sackcloth and clothed me with joy."

Psalm 30:11

Praise has the incredible power to transform our hearts and minds. When we lift our voices in worship, we invite God's presence into our situations, allowing His joy to replace our sadness and His peace to calm our worries. Praising God shifts our perspective and reminds us of His sovereignty, even in difficult times. This week, focus on how praise can bring about change in your emotional and spiritual state.

Prayer

Lord, help me to remember the power of praise in my life. Teach me how to turn my sorrows into songs of joy.

July 17

Praise in the Face of Adversity

"About midnight Paul and Silas were praying and singing hymns to God, and the other prisoners were listening to them."

Acts 16:25

The story of Paul and Silas illustrates the profound impact of praise, even in the darkest moments. Imprisoned for their faith, they chose to worship God in the midst of their trials. Their praise not only brought them peace but also served as a powerful witness to those around them. This week, consider how you can praise God in your own difficult situations, becoming a beacon of hope for others.

Reflect

What challenges are you currently facing? How can you incorporate praise into those situations to honor God and inspire others?

July 18

The Community of Praise

"I will declare Your name to my brothers and sisters; in the assembly, I will sing Your praises."

Hebrews 2:12

Praise is not only an individual act; it thrives in community. When we gather together to worship, we encourage one another and create an atmosphere of faith. The collective voices of praise unite us in purpose and strengthen our spirits. This week, consider how you can participate in communal worship, whether by attending a church service, joining a prayer group, or simply praising God with family and friends.

Prayer

Lord, thank You for the gift of community. Help me to be an active participant in praising You alongside others.

July 19

The Weapons of Praise

"Praise the Lord! For the Lord has heard my cry for mercy."

Psalm 28:6

Praise acts as a weapon against the enemy. When we declare God's goodness, we remind ourselves and those around us of His power over our lives and circumstances. Our praise can dismantle fear, anxiety, and doubt, replacing them with confidence and hope. This week, focus on using praise as a tool to combat negative thoughts and feelings, declaring God's truth over your life.

Reflect

What fears or doubts are holding you back? Write a

declaration of praise that counters those negative thoughts, affirming God's power and goodness.

July 20

A Lifestyle of Praise

"I will sing of Your love and justice; to You, Lord, I will sing praise."
Psalm 101:1

A lifestyle of praise means making worship a regular part of our daily routine. By incorporating praise into our day-to-day activities—through music, prayer, and gratitude—we cultivate a heart that continually seeks to honor God. This week, set aside specific times to engage in praise, whether it's singing in the car, thanking God during your morning routine, or sharing praises with others.

Prayer

Lord, help me to integrate praise into my daily life. Show me how to honor You in every moment.

July 21

The Joy of Praise

"You make known to me the path of life; You will fill me with joy in Your presence, with eternal pleasures at Your right hand."
Psalm 16:11

Ultimately, praise leads us to joy. When we focus on God's goodness and faithfulness, we are filled with a sense of joy and fulfillment that transcends our circumstances. In His presence, we find true joy, which sustains us through all of life's ups and downs. This week, embrace the joy that comes from praising God, allowing it to fill your heart and overflow into every aspect of your life.

Reflect

Reflect on a time when you experienced joy through praise. How can you seek that joy again this week as you focus on God's goodness?

Week 4: Worship and Surrender

Worship is an intimate act that goes beyond singing songs or attending church services; it encompasses our entire lives. True worship involves surrendering our will and desires to God, recognizing His sovereignty and goodness. This week, we will explore the profound connection between worship and surrender, discovering how laying down our lives before God can lead to deeper intimacy with Him and greater peace in our hearts.

July 22

The Heart of Surrender

"Therefore, I urge you, brothers and sisters, in view of God's mercy, to offer your bodies as a living sacrifice, holy and pleasing to God—this is your true and proper worship."

Romans 12:1

Surrender begins with recognizing God's mercy and grace in our lives. Paul encourages us to present ourselves as living sacrifices, which is the essence of true worship. This act of surrender requires us to let go of our own agendas and desires, placing God at the center of our lives. As we reflect on His love and mercy, we can find the strength to surrender our worries, fears, and ambitions to Him.

Reflect

What areas of your life are you struggling to surrender to God? Write a prayer of surrender, committing those areas to Him.

July 23

Surrendering Our Plans

"In their hearts, humans plan their course, but the Lord establishes their steps."

Proverbs 16:9

We often have our own plans for our lives, but surrendering those plans to God is essential for true worship. Trusting in His perfect timing and direction allows us to align our desires with His will. This week, consider how you can release your plans and expectations to God, trusting that He knows what is best for you. Worship is a way to acknowledge His authority over our lives and embrace the journey He has for us.

Prayer

Lord, help me to trust You with my plans. I surrender my desires to You, knowing that Your ways are higher than mine.

July 24

Worshiping Through Uncertainty

"Trust in the Lord with all your heart and lean not on your own understanding; in all your ways submit to Him, and He will make your paths straight."

Proverbs 3:5-6

Life is often filled with uncertainties, but worshiping God

in these moments can provide clarity and peace. When we surrender our understanding and trust in God, we allow Him to lead us through our confusion. This week, focus on how you can worship God in your uncertainty, seeking His guidance and peace as you navigate life's challenges.

Reflect

What uncertainties are you facing right now? How can you seek God's guidance through worship and prayer during this time?

July 25

The Beauty of Surrender

"When Jesus had finished saying these things, the crowds were amazed at His teaching."

Matthew 7:28

Jesus modeled surrender perfectly in His life, especially in the Garden of Gethsemane, where He prayed, "Not my will, but Yours be done." Surrendering to God is an act of worship that acknowledges His authority and goodness. When we surrender, we open ourselves to receive His guidance and blessings. This week, meditate on the beauty of surrender and how it can lead to a deeper understanding of God's will for your life.

Prayer

Lord, help me to see surrender not as a loss but as a beautiful act of trust in You. Teach me to embrace Your will with an open heart.

July 26

Surrendering Our Fears

"So do not fear, for I am with you; do not be dismayed, for I am your God. I will strengthen you and help you; I will uphold you with my righteous right hand."
Isaiah 41:10

Fear can be a significant barrier to surrender. When we hold onto our fears, we are unable to fully worship God and trust in His promises. Surrendering our fears allows us to experience His presence and strength in our lives. This week, take time to identify the fears that are holding you back, and offer them to God in worship. Allow His perfect love to cast out fear and fill you with peace.

Reflect

Write down your fears and pray over them, surrendering each one to God and trusting Him to provide strength and courage.

July 27

The Freedom of Surrender

"It is for freedom that Christ has set us free; stand firm, then, and do not let yourselves be burdened again by a yoke of slavery."
Galatians 5:1

Surrendering to God leads to true freedom. When we release our burdens and allow Him to carry them, we experience the peace and joy that come from walking in His will. Worshiping through surrender can free us from the weight of expectations, regrets, and the need for control. This week, reflect on how surrendering your burdens to God can lead to greater freedom in your life.

Prayer

Lord, thank You for the freedom You offer through surrender. Help me to let go of my burdens and experience the joy of walking in Your grace.

July 28

A Lifestyle of Worship and Surrender

"Submit yourselves, then, to God. Resist the devil, and he will flee from you."

James 4:7

Worship and surrender are intertwined; both are vital for living a life that glorifies God. Embracing a lifestyle of worship means continually surrendering our hearts, minds, and lives to Him. This week, consider practical ways you can incorporate worship and surrender into your daily routine. Whether it's through prayer, music, or serving others, look for opportunities to honor God with your whole being.

Reflect

How can you make worship and surrender a consistent part of your life? Write down specific actions you can take to cultivate this lifestyle.

8

August

Week 1: Developing Spiritual Disciplines

Spiritual disciplines are intentional practices that cultivate a deeper relationship with God and help us grow in our faith. They provide structure and guidance for our spiritual journey, allowing us to connect with God in meaningful ways. This week, we will explore various spiritual disciplines, emphasizing their importance in nurturing our relationship with God and enhancing our spiritual lives.

August 1

The Importance of Spiritual Disciplines

"Discipline yourself for the purpose of godliness."

1 Timothy 4:7

Spiritual disciplines are vital for our growth in faith. They help us cultivate habits that align our hearts and minds with God's will. Just as physical disciplines like exercise and diet are essential for our physical health, spiritual disciplines are necessary for our spiritual well-being. This week, reflect on how incorporating spiritual practices into your daily life can deepen your relationship with God and help you grow in godliness.

Reflect

What spiritual disciplines have you practiced in the past? Which ones do you feel called to explore further?

August 2

The Discipline of Prayer

"Pray without ceasing."
1 Thessalonians 5:17

Prayer is a foundational spiritual discipline that connects us with God. It is through prayer that we communicate with Him, seek His guidance, and express our needs and gratitude. This week, consider how you can develop a consistent prayer life. Set aside specific times for prayer, and experiment with different forms of prayer—adoration, confession, thanksgiving, and supplication—to deepen your experience with God.

Prayer

Lord, help me to prioritize prayer in my life. Teach me to communicate with You regularly and honestly.

August 3

The Discipline of Scripture Reading

"Your word is a lamp to my feet and a light to my path."
Psalm 119:105

Reading and meditating on Scripture is another essential discipline that nourishes our souls and guides our actions. The Bible reveals God's character, His promises, and His will for our lives. This week, commit to reading a portion of Scripture daily, allowing it to inform your thoughts and decisions. Consider using a journal to reflect on what you read and how it applies to your life.

Reflect

What passage of Scripture resonates with you today? How can you apply its teachings to your life?

August 4

The Discipline of Worship

"God is spirit, and those who worship Him must worship in spirit and truth."

John 4:24

Worship is an essential spiritual discipline that involves honoring God through our thoughts, words, and actions. It is not confined to a church service; worship can be expressed in our daily lives as we acknowledge God's presence and greatness. This week, find opportunities to worship God throughout your day, whether through music, gratitude, or acts of service.

Prayer

Lord, help me to cultivate a heart of worship. Teach me to recognize Your presence in every moment and respond with gratitude and praise.

August 5

The Discipline of Fasting

"But He said to them, 'This kind does not go out except by prayer

and fasting.'"
Matthew 17:21

Fasting is a spiritual discipline that encourages us to seek God more earnestly by temporarily giving up something, often food, to focus on prayer and spiritual growth. It serves as a reminder of our dependence on God. This week, consider setting aside a meal or another activity to dedicate time to prayer and reflection. Use this time to draw closer to God and seek His guidance.

Reflect

What might you fast from this week to deepen your relationship with God? How can this discipline enhance your spiritual journey?

August 6

The Discipline of Fellowship

"And let us consider how to stir up one another to love and good works, not neglecting to meet together, as is the habit of some, but encouraging one another, and all the more as you see the Day drawing near."
Hebrews 10:24-25

Fellowship with other believers is a crucial discipline that strengthens our faith. Engaging with others in spiritual conversations, worship, and community encourages us and holds us accountable in our walk with Christ. This week, reach out to fellow believers to share your faith journey, join a Bible study, or participate in a small group.

Prayer

Lord, thank You for the gift of community. Help me to seek

and nurture relationships that encourage spiritual growth.

August 7

The Discipline of Service

"Each of you should use whatever gift you have received to serve others, as faithful stewards of God's grace in its various forms."
1 Peter 4:10

Serving others is an expression of our love for God and a vital spiritual discipline. When we serve, we reflect Christ's heart and share His love with the world. This week, look for ways to serve those around you, whether through acts of kindness, volunteering, or simply being present for someone in need.

Reflect

What gifts or talents has God given you to use in service? How can you apply these in your community this week?

Week 2: Growing in Prayer

Prayer is a vital lifeline for believers, serving as a means of communication with God and a pathway to deeper intimacy with Him. This week, we will focus on the importance of growing in our prayer life, exploring different aspects of prayer, and learning how to cultivate a consistent and meaningful practice of connecting with God.

August 8

Understanding the Purpose of Prayer

"And this is the confidence that we have toward Him, that if we ask anything according to His will, He hears us."

1 John 5:14

Prayer is not merely about asking for things; it is an opportunity to align our hearts with God's will and purposes. Understanding the purpose of prayer helps us approach it with the right mindset. It is a chance to express our desires, seek guidance, and cultivate a relationship with our Creator. This week, reflect on the various reasons for prayer: to praise God, confess our sins, express gratitude, and intercede for others.

Reflect

Write down your understanding of prayer. What do you hope to achieve or experience in your prayer life?

August 9

Building a Consistent Prayer Habit

"Devote yourselves to prayer, being watchful and thankful."
Colossians 4:2

Consistency in prayer is key to spiritual growth. Just as we develop habits in other areas of our lives, cultivating a habit of prayer requires intentionality. This week, set aside specific times each day to pray, whether it's in the morning, during lunch, or before bed. Create a prayer schedule that works for you, and be watchful for opportunities to connect with God throughout your day.

Prayer

Lord, help me to develop a consistent prayer habit. May my heart be devoted to seeking You daily.

August 10

Types of Prayer

"Pray in the Spirit on all occasions with all kinds of prayers and requests."
Ephesians 6:18

There are various types of prayer, each serving a unique purpose. This week, explore different forms of prayer, including:

- **Adoration**: Praising God for who He is.
- **Confession**: Acknowledging our sins and seeking forgiveness.
- **Thanksgiving**: Expressing gratitude for God's blessings.
- **Supplication**: Bringing our requests and the needs of others before God.

Consider incorporating these types of prayer into your daily practice to enrich your conversation with God.

Reflect

Which type of prayer resonates with you the most? How can you integrate more variety into your prayer life?

August 11

Praying with Scripture

"I have hidden Your word in my heart that I might not sin against You."
Psalm 119:11

Praying through Scripture is a powerful way to deepen your prayer life. By meditating on God's Word, you can pray His promises and truths back to Him. This week, choose a passage from the Bible and use it as a foundation for your prayers. Let the words inspire your requests and praises, allowing Scripture to guide your conversations with God.

Prayer

Lord, help me to incorporate Your Word into my prayers. May Your Scriptures come alive in my heart and guide my conversations with You.

August 12

The Power of Intercessory Prayer

"I urge, then, first of all, that petitions, prayers, intercession, and thanksgiving be made for all people."

1 Timothy 2:1

Intercessory prayer involves praying for the needs of others, standing in the gap on their behalf. This week, focus on the power of intercession. Make a list of people or situations you want to pray for, and dedicate specific time to lift them up in prayer. As you intercede for others, remember that God hears and responds to our prayers, and your intercession can have a profound impact on their lives.

Reflect

Who in your life needs your prayers right now? How can you actively support them through intercessory prayer?

August 13

Overcoming Barriers to Prayer

"You do not have because you do not ask."

James 4:2

Many believers face barriers to prayer, such as distractions, doubt, or a lack of confidence. Identifying these barriers is the first step in overcoming them. This week, take time to reflect on what hinders your prayer life and consider practical steps to address these challenges. Create a distraction-free environment for prayer, remind yourself of God's faithfulness, and approach Him with confidence and humility.

Prayer

Lord, reveal to me the barriers in my prayer life. Help me to overcome them and draw closer to You through prayer.

Augusy 14

The Joy of Prayer

"Rejoice always, pray continually, give thanks in all circumstances; for this is God's will for you in Christ Jesus."
1 Thessalonians 5:16-18

Prayer brings joy and peace, grounding us in God's presence amid life's challenges. As you conclude this week, take time to reflect on the joy that comes from spending time in prayer. Celebrate the answered prayers, the lessons learned, and the closeness you've experienced with God. Make a commitment to continue growing in your prayer life, knowing that it is a journey filled with blessings and transformation.

Reflect

How has your understanding of prayer changed this week? What commitments will you make to continue growing in your prayer life?

Week 3: Diving Deeper into God's Word

God's Word is a rich source of wisdom, guidance, and nourishment for our souls. This week, we will focus on how to dive deeper into the Scriptures, discovering the transformative power of studying and applying God's Word to our lives. By immersing ourselves in the Bible, we can grow in understanding and strengthen our relationship with God.

August 15

The Importance of God's Word

"For the word of God is alive and active. Sharper than any double-edged sword, it penetrates even to dividing soul and spirit, joints and marrow; it judges the thoughts and attitudes of the heart."

Hebrews 4:12

God's Word is not just a collection of ancient texts; it is alive and powerful, capable of transforming our hearts and minds. Understanding the importance of Scripture in our spiritual journey is crucial for our growth. This week, reflect on how you have experienced the impact of God's Word in your life and how it has shaped your faith.

Reflect

How has the Word of God influenced your life? Write about a specific instance where a verse or passage spoke to you.

August 16

Approaching Scripture with an Open Heart

"Open my eyes that I may see wonderful things in Your law."

Psalm 119:18

To dive deeper into God's Word, we must approach it with an open heart and a desire to learn. Prayerfully ask God to reveal His truths as you read and meditate on Scripture. This week, set aside time to read a passage of your choice and invite the Holy Spirit to illuminate your understanding. Journaling your thoughts and insights can also help deepen your comprehension.

Prayer

Lord, help me to approach Your Word with an open heart. Reveal Your truths to me and guide my understanding as I read.

August 17

Methods for Studying the Bible

"Study to show yourself approved unto God, a workman that needeth not to be ashamed, rightly dividing the word of truth."
2 Timothy 2:15

Studying the Bible involves more than just reading it; it requires intention and focus. This week, explore different methods for studying Scripture, such as:

- **Verse Mapping**: Breaking down a verse to understand its meaning and context.
- **Topical Studies**: Exploring specific themes or topics throughout the Bible.
- **Inductive Study**: Observing, interpreting, and applying passages through a systematic approach.

Experiment with these methods to see which resonates with you and enhances your understanding of God's Word.

Reflect

Which study method do you want to try this week? How do you think it will help you dive deeper into Scripture?

August 18

Memorizing Scripture

"I have hidden Your word in my heart that I might not sin against You."

Psalm 119:11

Memorizing Scripture is a powerful discipline that allows God's Word to dwell within us. By committing verses to memory, we can recall them in times of need, offering us guidance, comfort, and strength. This week, choose a verse or passage to memorize and find creative ways to incorporate it into your daily life, such as writing it on sticky notes or using flashcards.

Prayer

Lord, help me to hide Your Word in my heart. May it guide my thoughts and actions as I seek to live according to Your will.

August 19

The Context of Scripture

"For precept must be upon precept, precept upon precept; line upon line, line upon line; here a little, and there a little."

Isaiah 28:10

Understanding the context of Scripture is essential for accurate interpretation. This week, as you study, pay attention to the historical and cultural background of the passages you read.

Consider who wrote the text, to whom it was addressed, and the circumstances surrounding it. This deeper understanding will enrich your insights and help you apply God's Word more effectively in your life.

Reflect

What context have you learned about a specific passage recently? How has it changed your understanding of that Scripture?

August 20

Applying God's Word to Your Life

"Do not merely listen to the word, and so deceive yourselves. Do what it says."

James 1:22

Studying God's Word is not just an intellectual exercise; it is meant to transform our lives. This week, focus on how you can apply what you learn from Scripture in your daily life. Look for opportunities to live out the principles you discover, whether in your relationships, work, or personal growth.

Prayer

Lord, help me not only to learn Your Word but to live it out in my life. Show me how to apply Your truths in practical ways.

August 21

The Joy of Community and Discussion

"Iron sharpens iron, and one man sharpens another."

Proverbs 27:17

Studying Scripture is a rich experience that can be enhanced through community. Engaging in discussions with fellow believers allows us to gain different perspectives and insights. This week, consider joining a Bible study group or finding a friend to discuss what you've learned. Sharing your thoughts and hearing others can deepen your understanding and encourage accountability.

Reflect

Who can you share your insights with this week? How can discussing Scripture with others enhance your learning?

Week 4: Bearing Spiritual Fruit

As followers of Christ, we are called to bear fruit that reflects our relationship with Him. This week, we will explore the significance of spiritual fruit in our lives, what it means to cultivate these qualities, and how they can impact our relationships with God and others. By understanding and practicing the fruits of the Spirit, we can live out our faith authentically and impact the world around us.

August 22

Understanding Spiritual Fruit

"But the fruit of the Spirit is love, joy, peace, forbearance, kindness, goodness, faithfulness, gentleness and self-control."
Galatians 5:22-23

Spiritual fruit is the visible evidence of a believer's relationship with Christ. The fruit of the Spirit reflects His character and is produced in our lives through the work of the Holy Spirit. This week, take time to meditate on each aspect of the fruit of the Spirit and how they manifest in your life. Recognizing these traits can help you identify areas where God is working in you.

Reflect

Which of the fruits of the Spirit do you feel is most evident in your life? Which one do you desire to cultivate more?

August 23

The Importance of Love

"And above all these put on love, which binds everything together in perfect harmony."
Colossians 3:14

Love is the foundation of the Christian life and the first fruit of the Spirit. It is the driving force behind our actions and interactions with others. This week, focus on how you can demonstrate Christ-like love in your relationships, whether through acts of service, words of affirmation, or simply being present for someone in need.

Prayer

Lord, help me to love others as You love me. Show me ways to demonstrate Your love in my daily interactions.

August 24

Cultivating Joy and Peace

"You make known to me the path of life; in Your presence, there is fullness of joy; at Your right hand are pleasures forevermore."
Psalm 16:11

Joy and peace are essential fruits that reflect our trust in God. Joy is not dependent on our circumstances but is rooted in our relationship with Him. Similarly, peace is a gift from God that guards our hearts and minds. This week, seek to cultivate joy and peace by spending time in God's presence, meditating on His promises, and practicing gratitude for the blessings in your life.

Reflect

What practices help you experience joy and peace in your life? How can you prioritize these in your daily routine?

August 25

Practicing Kindness and Goodness

"And let us not grow weary of doing good, for in due season we will reap, if we do not give up."

Galatians 6:9

Kindness and goodness are outward expressions of the love of Christ in our lives. They involve actively seeking to benefit others and reflecting God's character in our actions. This week, look for opportunities to perform acts of kindness, whether large or small. Consider how you can extend goodness to those around you, both in your words and actions.

Prayer

Lord, help me to be a vessel of kindness and goodness. Open my eyes to the needs of others, and give me the courage to respond.

August 26

Faithfulness and Gentleness

"The one who calls you is faithful, and He will do it."

1 Thessalonians 5:24

Faithfulness and gentleness are important characteristics of a believer. Faithfulness involves being reliable and trustworthy, while gentleness reflects humility and a soft approach in our interactions with others. This week, examine areas where you can demonstrate faithfulness to God's calling and gentleness in your relationships. Consider how these qualities can be a testimony to others of Christ's love.

Reflect

In what areas of your life do you need to show more faithfulness or gentleness? How can you actively work on these traits this week?

August 27

Developing Self-Control

"For God gave us a spirit not of fear but of power and love and self-control."

2 Timothy 1:7

Self-control is an essential fruit of the Spirit that empowers us to resist temptation and make choices that honor God. It requires discipline and reliance on the Holy Spirit. This week, identify areas in your life where self-control is needed, whether in your habits, relationships, or reactions to challenges. Seek God's help in developing this fruit, knowing that He gives us strength to overcome.

Prayer

Lord, help me to practice self-control in all areas of my life. Strengthen me to resist temptation and choose what honors You.

August 28

Reflecting on Your Spiritual Fruit

"By this My Father is glorified, that you bear much fruit and so prove to be My disciples."
John 15:8

As this week concludes, take time to reflect on the spiritual fruit in your life. Consider how you have seen the fruit of the Spirit manifest in your thoughts, actions, and relationships. Celebrate the progress you have made and ask God to continue cultivating these qualities within you. Remember that bearing spiritual fruit is not just for your benefit but is a testament to God's work in your life.

Reflect

How have you seen the fruit of the Spirit grow in your life this week? What will you commit to doing to continue bearing fruit in the future?

9

September

Week 1: Discovering God's Purpose for Your Life

Understanding God's purpose for your life is a transformative journey that can lead to fulfillment, joy, and a deeper relationship with Him. This week, we will explore the steps to discern and embrace the unique calling that God has placed on your life. As you engage with Scripture and reflect on your experiences, you will begin to uncover the beautiful plans God has for you.

September 1

Seeking God's Will

"For I know the plans I have for you," declares the Lord, "plans to prosper you and not to harm you, plans to give you hope and a future."

Jeremiah 29:11

The journey to discovering God's purpose begins with seeking

Him wholeheartedly. God assures us that He has good plans for our lives. This week, commit to spending intentional time in prayer, asking God to reveal His will for you. Open your heart to His guidance, and be ready to listen for His direction in your life.

Reflect

What does seeking God's will mean to you? How can you prioritize your time with God this week?

September 2

Understanding Your Gifts and Talents

"Each of you should use whatever gift you have received to serve others, as faithful stewards of God's grace in its various forms."

1 Peter 4:10

God has uniquely gifted each of us for His purpose. Understanding your spiritual gifts and natural talents is essential for discerning your calling. This week, take time to identify your strengths and passions. Consider how these can be used to serve others and glorify God. You might take a spiritual gifts assessment or simply reflect on the activities that bring you joy and fulfillment.

Prayer

Lord, help me to recognize the gifts and talents You have given me. Show me how I can use them for Your glory and the good of others.

September 3

Reflecting on Your Life Experiences

"And we know that in all things God works for the good of those who love Him, who have been called according to His purpose."

Romans 8:28

Our life experiences shape us and play a significant role in revealing God's purpose. This week, reflect on the key moments in your life—both the triumphs and the trials. Consider how God has worked through those experiences to prepare you for your calling. Understanding your past can provide insight into how God may want to use you in the future.

Reflect

What significant experiences have shaped your life? How might they contribute to your understanding of God's purpose for you?

September 4

Listening to God's Voice

"My sheep hear My voice, and I know them, and they follow Me."
John 10:27

Listening to God is crucial in discovering His purpose. This week, practice tuning in to His voice through prayer, meditation, and reading Scripture. Ask the Holy Spirit to guide you and provide clarity regarding your path. Pay attention to any thoughts, feelings, or insights that arise during your quiet time with God.

Prayer

Lord, I want to hear Your voice clearly. Help me to discern Your guidance and be sensitive to the promptings of Your Spirit.

September 5

Seeking Counsel from Others

"Plans fail for lack of counsel, but with many advisers they succeed."

Proverbs 15:22

God often speaks through the wisdom of others. This week, consider reaching out to trusted friends, mentors, or spiritual leaders who can offer guidance and perspective as you seek to understand your purpose. Discuss your thoughts and feelings with them and be open to their insights.

Reflect

Who in your life can provide counsel as you seek to discover God's purpose? How can you initiate a conversation with them this week?

September 6

Embracing the Journey of Discovery

"Delight yourself in the Lord, and He will give you the desires of your heart."

Psalm 37:4

Discovering God's purpose is not always an instant revelation; it is a journey that unfolds over time. This week, embrace the process of exploration and growth. Be patient and trust that God is working in your heart, shaping your desires to align with His will. Enjoy the moments of discovery and be open to the surprises along the way.

Prayer

Lord, help me to embrace the journey of discovering Your purpose for my life. Teach me to trust in Your timing and to delight in the process.

September 7

Taking Steps of Faith

"Now faith is confidence in what we hope for and assurance about what we do not see."

Hebrews 11:1

As you conclude this week, reflect on what you have learned about God's purpose for your life. Consider taking steps of faith based on what you have discerned. It might involve volunteering, pursuing a new opportunity, or sharing your gifts with others. Remember that each step, no matter how small, brings you closer to fulfilling the calling God has placed on your life.

Reflect

What specific steps can you take this week to align with God's purpose for you? How can you act in faith as you move forward?

Week 2: Serving Others with Your Gifts

God has uniquely equipped each of us with talents, abilities, and spiritual gifts, not only for our personal growth but to serve others and build His kingdom. This week, we will explore how to use the gifts God has given us to bless those around us and make an impact for Christ. By aligning our gifts with a heart of service, we can live out our purpose and reflect God's love to the world.

September 8

Identifying Your Gifts

"We have different gifts, according to the grace given to each of us."
Romans 12:6

Every believer has been given unique gifts by God to serve others. These gifts are not only for personal use but are meant to bless the community and bring glory to God. This week, reflect on the specific gifts, skills, and passions you have been given. Consider how these can be used in service to others.

Reflect

What gifts and talents has God given you? How can you begin using them to serve those around you?

September 9

Serving with a Humble Heart

"Each of you should use whatever gift you have received to serve others, as faithful stewards of God's grace in its various forms."
1 Peter 4:10

Serving others begins with a heart of humility. Recognize that the gifts you possess are a reflection of God's grace and are meant to benefit others, not for self-promotion. This week, pray for a humble heart as you seek to serve. Look for opportunities to serve others quietly, without seeking recognition, and trust that God sees your efforts.

Prayer

Lord, help me to serve others with humility. Let my actions reflect Your grace and love, and may I always give You the glory.

September 10

Serving in Your Community

"For even the Son of Man did not come to be served, but to serve, and to give His life as a ransom for many."
Mark 10:45

Jesus is our ultimate example of selfless service. He gave His life to serve others, and we are called to follow in His footsteps. This week, think about how you can serve your local community. Whether through your church, a nonprofit, or a simple act of kindness to a neighbor, look for ways to use your gifts to meet the needs of others around you.

Reflect

What are the needs in your community? How can you use your gifts to make a difference?

September 11

The Joy of Serving Others

"It is more blessed to give than to receive."
Acts 20:35

Serving others brings joy, not only to those we serve but also to us. There is a unique blessing in giving of our time, energy, and talents to help others. This week, reflect on the joy that comes from serving. Pay attention to how you feel when you use your gifts for God's kingdom, and embrace the joy that follows selfless service.

Prayer

Lord, thank You for the joy that comes from serving others. Help me to give generously and experience the blessing of selfless service.

September 12

Serving Through Small Acts of Kindness

"Do not neglect to do good and to share what you have, for such sacrifices are pleasing to God."

Hebrews 13:16

Sometimes serving doesn't require grand gestures—it can be as simple as an encouraging word, a kind deed, or lending a helping hand. This week, focus on small, daily acts of kindness. Whether it's helping a coworker, supporting a friend in need, or even just offering a smile, each small act of service reflects God's love.

Reflect

What small acts of kindness can you offer to others this week? How can you be intentional in serving through everyday moments?

September 13

Overcoming the Fear of Serving

"For God has not given us a spirit of fear, but of power and of love and of a sound mind."

2 Timothy 1:7

Sometimes fear or insecurity can hold us back from serving others. We might feel unqualified or worry about how others will perceive us. This week, ask God to help you overcome any fear or doubt that is stopping you from serving. Remember that God empowers you, and your willingness to serve is more important than perfection.

Prayer

Lord, remove any fear or doubt that holds me back from

serving others. Give me boldness and confidence to step out and use my gifts for Your glory.

September 14

Finding Fulfillment in Service

"Whatever you do, work heartily, as for the Lord and not for men."
Colossians 3:23

True fulfillment comes from serving God through the gifts He has given you. As you conclude this week, reflect on how serving others has deepened your faith and brought you closer to God. Remember that every act of service, no matter how big or small, is an offering to God. Continue to seek opportunities to serve and find joy in using your gifts for His kingdom.

Reflect

How has serving others this week brought you closer to God? What steps can you take to continue serving with joy and purpose?

Week 3: Living Out Your Calling

Once you have discovered your gifts and understood God's purpose for your life, the next step is to actively live out that calling. Living out your calling means walking in obedience to God's direction and faithfully using the gifts He has given you for His glory. This week, we will explore what it means to live out your calling with confidence, consistency, and trust in God's leading.

September 15

Stepping Out in Faith

"The Lord had said to Abram, 'Go from your country, your people and your father's household to the land I will show you.'"

Genesis 12:1

Living out your calling often requires stepping into the unknown. Just as Abraham was called to leave his familiar surroundings to follow God, we too must take steps of faith when God calls us. This week, focus on trusting God with the steps He is leading you to take, even if you cannot see the full picture. He will guide you as you follow Him in faith.

Reflect

What is one area of your life where you need to take a step of faith? How can you trust God's leading even when the way seems uncertain?

September 16

Obeying God's Call

"If you are willing and obedient, you will eat the good things of the land."

Isaiah 1:19

Obedience is key to living out your calling. Sometimes, God's instructions may seem challenging or unclear, but when we trust and obey, we experience the fullness of His blessings. This week, pray for the strength to walk in obedience, knowing that God's plans are good. Reflect on areas where God is calling you to take action, and commit to following His lead.

prayer

Lord, give me the courage to obey Your call, even when it's difficult. Help me to trust that Your plans are always for my good.

September 17

Overcoming Challenges in Your Calling

"Consider it pure joy, my brothers and sisters, whenever you face trials of many kinds, because you know that the testing of your faith produces perseverance."

James 1:2-3

Living out your calling doesn't mean the road will always be easy. Challenges, setbacks, and opposition are part of the journey. But these trials can strengthen your faith and refine your character. This week, reflect on any obstacles you are facing in your calling. Ask God to help you persevere and remain faithful in the midst of challenges, trusting that He is with you every step of the way.

Reflect

What challenges are you facing as you live out your calling? How can you view these challenges as opportunities for growth?

September 18

Staying Faithful in the Small Things

"Whoever can be trusted with very little can also be trusted with much."

Luke 16:10

God often calls us to be faithful in small tasks before entrusting us with greater responsibilities. Living out your calling doesn't always mean doing big things right away; sometimes it means being consistent and diligent in the everyday moments. This week, focus on being faithful in the small things God has placed in your path, trusting that He will prepare you for greater things in His time.

Prayer

Lord, help me to be faithful in the small tasks You have given me. Teach me to serve with joy and diligence, trusting that You are preparing me for more.

September 19

Trusting God's Timing

"He has made everything beautiful in its time."
Ecclesiastes 3:11

One of the hardest parts of living out your calling is waiting on God's timing. You may feel ready to move forward, but God's timing may not align with your own. This week, reflect on areas where you need to trust God's perfect timing. Be patient and rest in the knowledge that God is working behind the scenes, preparing you and the circumstances around you for what's next.

Reflect

Are there areas of your calling where you feel impatient? How can you trust that God's timing is perfect, even when you don't understand it?

September 20

Using Your Calling to Impact Others

"In the same way, let your light shine before others, that they may see your good deeds and glorify your Father in heaven."
Matthew 5:16

Your calling is not just for you—it's meant to impact the lives of others. When you live out your calling, you become a light that reflects God's love, grace, and truth to those around you. This week, focus on how you can use your gifts and calling to serve and uplift others. Whether through acts of service, words of encouragement, or simply sharing your testimony, your calling can make a difference in the lives of those you encounter.

Prayer

Lord, help me to use my calling to impact others for Your glory. Open my eyes to the needs around me, and give me the courage to be a light in the lives of others.

September 21

Finding Joy in Your Calling

"For we are God's handiwork, created in Christ Jesus to do good works, which God prepared in advance for us to do."

Ephesians 2:10

Living out your calling is not a burden; it's a source of deep joy and fulfillment. As you conclude this week, reflect on the joy that comes from knowing you are walking in the path God has prepared for you. Celebrate the unique way God has called and equipped you, and find joy in the journey of living out your purpose each day.

Reflect

How has living out your calling brought you joy this week? What can you do to continue finding joy in following God's plan for your life?

Week 4: Trusting God with Your Future

Trusting God with your future is a vital part of living out your calling. We may not always know what the future holds, but we can trust the One who holds the future. This week, we will explore how to surrender our plans to God, trust His direction, and have confidence in His promises for our future. By letting go of control and placing our trust in God, we experience peace and assurance in His perfect plan for our lives.

September 22

Surrendering Your Plans to God

"Commit to the Lord whatever you do, and He will establish your plans."

Proverbs 16:3

Trusting God with your future begins with surrendering your plans to Him. While it's natural to have hopes and dreams, it's essential to submit them to God's will. This week, take time to lay your plans, desires, and ambitions before God. Trust that His plans for you are good and that He knows what is best for your future.

Prayer

Lord, I surrender my plans and desires to You. Help me to trust that Your plans for my future are far better than anything I could imagine.

September 23

Trusting God in Uncertainty

"Trust in the Lord with all your heart and lean not on your own understanding."

Proverbs 3:5

Life is full of uncertainties, and it's easy to feel anxious about the unknown. However, God calls us to trust Him even when we don't understand what's happening. This week, focus on releasing your need for control and trusting God in times of uncertainty. Know that He is guiding you, even when the path ahead is unclear.

Reflect

In what areas of your life do you feel uncertain about the future? How can you trust God's guidance during times of uncertainty?

September 24

God's Promises for Your Future

"For I know the plans I have for you," declares the Lord, "plans to prosper you and not to harm you, plans to give you hope and a future."

Jeremiah 29:11

God's Word is filled with promises about our future. He assures us that He has good plans for us—plans filled with hope. This week, meditate on the promises of God for your future. Let them be a source of comfort and encouragement as you navigate life's uncertainties, knowing that God's plans for you are always for your good.

Prayer

Lord, thank You for Your promises for my future. Help me to hold on to Your Word and trust that You are leading me toward a future filled with hope and purpose.

September 25

Trusting God with Your Timing

"Wait for the Lord; be strong and take heart and wait for the Lord."

Psalm 27:14

Trusting God with your future often involves waiting on His timing. It can be difficult to be patient when you're eager for something to happen, but God's timing is always perfect. This week, focus on trusting God's timing, even when it seems slow or uncertain. Be encouraged that He is at work behind the scenes, preparing you for what's ahead.

Reflect

Are there areas in your life where you are struggling to wait on God's timing? How can you practice patience and trust in His perfect timing?

September 26

Letting Go of Fear About the Future

"So do not fear, for I am with you; do not be dismayed, for I am your God. I will strengthen you and help you; I will uphold you with my righteous right hand."

Isaiah 41:10

Fear of the unknown can prevent us from trusting God fully. However, God promises that He is with us, no matter what the future holds. This week, focus on letting go of any fears or anxieties you have about the future. Trust that God is with you, guiding and protecting you, and that He will strengthen you through every challenge ahead.

Prayer

Lord, help me to release my fears about the future. Remind

me that You are always with me, and I can trust You to guide me through whatever comes my way.

September 27

Following God's Leading

"The Lord will guide you always; He will satisfy your needs in a sun-scorched land and will strengthen your frame."
Isaiah 58:11

God promises to guide us as we seek His will for our lives. Trusting God with your future means being open to His leading, even when it takes you in unexpected directions. This week, commit to listening for God's guidance through prayer and Scripture. Trust that He will lead you on the path that brings the most glory to Him and fulfillment to you.

Reflect

How can you be more attentive to God's leading in your life? What steps can you take to follow His direction with trust and confidence?

September 28

Finding Peace in God's Plan

"You will keep in perfect peace those whose minds are steadfast, because they trust in you."
Isaiah 26:3

As you conclude this week, reflect on the peace that comes from trusting God with your future. When you place your trust in God and surrender control, you can experience a sense of calm and confidence, knowing that He holds your life in His hands. Embrace the peace that comes from knowing that

God's plans for you are good, and He will never lead you astray.

Prayer

Lord, thank You for the peace that comes from trusting You with my future. Help me to keep my mind steadfast on You, and let me rest in the assurance that Your plans for me are perfect.

10

October

Week 1: Overcoming Weakness

We all experience moments of weakness—whether physical, emotional, or spiritual. But the Bible reassures us that in our weakest moments, God's strength shines the brightest. Overcoming weakness isn't about eliminating every frailty or struggle but learning to lean on God's strength and grace in the midst of them. This week, we will explore how God's power is made perfect in our weakness and how we can overcome our limitations by relying on His strength.

October 1

God's Strength in Our Weakness

"But He said to me, 'My grace is sufficient for you, for My power is made perfect in weakness.' Therefore I will boast all the more gladly about my weaknesses, so that Christ's power may rest on me."

2 Corinthians 12:9

In a culture that values strength and self-sufficiency, weakness can feel like something to hide or overcome on our own. But in God's kingdom, weakness is an opportunity for His power to be displayed in our lives. This week, start by embracing your areas of weakness, knowing that God's grace is sufficient. When you feel weak, it's an invitation to rely more fully on God's strength.

Reflect

What weaknesses or struggles do you face today? How can you invite God's power into those areas of your life?

October 2

Relying on God's Grace

"Let us then approach God's throne of grace with confidence, so that we may receive mercy and find grace to help us in our time of need."

Hebrews 4:16

We all have moments when we feel overwhelmed by our weaknesses. But instead of trying to handle it all on your own, God invites you to come to Him with confidence. His grace is abundant and always available to help you in your time of need. This week, make a habit of turning to God for help, instead of relying on your own strength. He will supply you with the grace and strength you need.

Prayer

Lord, I confess my weakness and my need for You. Help me to trust in Your grace and strength instead of my own abilities.

October 3

The Power of Humility

"Humble yourselves before the Lord, and He will lift you up."
James 4:10

Humility is the key to overcoming weakness. When we humble ourselves before God and acknowledge that we can't do it all on our own, we open the door for Him to lift us up. This week, reflect on the areas where you've been trying to handle things in your own strength. Ask God to give you a heart of humility, so you can fully depend on His strength.

Reflect

In what areas of your life do you need to embrace humility and stop relying on your own strength? How can you invite God to lift you up in those moments?

October 4

Overcoming Fear of Weakness

"So do not fear, for I am with you; do not be dismayed, for I am your God. I will strengthen you and help you; I will uphold you with my righteous right hand."
Isaiah 41:10

It's easy to fear our own weaknesses—fear of failure, fear of rejection, fear of inadequacy. But God reminds us that we don't need to be afraid. He promises to strengthen us, help us, and uphold us. This week, focus on letting go of the fear of your weaknesses and embracing God's promise to be with you, strengthening and guiding you through every challenge.

Prayer

Lord, help me to release the fear of my weaknesses and trust that You are my strength. Remind me that with You by my side, I have nothing to fear.

October 5

Strength in Community

"Carry each other's burdens, and in this way you will fulfill the law of Christ."

Galatians 6:2

One of the ways God helps us overcome weakness is through community. We aren't meant to carry our burdens alone. This week, focus on the people God has placed in your life to support and encourage you. Whether through prayer, friendship, or a listening ear, God often uses others to strengthen us in our weak moments. Be open to receiving help and also be willing to offer it to others.

Reflect

Who are the people in your life that support you in your weak moments? How can you lean on and strengthen your community as you overcome challenges together?

October 6

Persevering in Weakness

"Let us not become weary in doing good, for at the proper time we will reap a harvest if we do not give up."

Galatians 6:9

Overcoming weakness is often a process that requires perseverance. You may not see immediate change or feel instantly strong, but God calls us to keep going. This week, focus on perseverance—pressing forward in faith, even when you feel weak or discouraged. Trust that God is working in you, and He will bring about growth and strength in time.

Prayer

Lord, give me the perseverance to keep going, even when I feel weak. Help me to trust that You are strengthening me, and give me the endurance to keep moving forward.

October 7

Victory Through Christ

"I can do all this through Him who gives me strength."
Philippians 4:13

As you conclude this week, reflect on the victory you have in Christ. You don't have to overcome weakness on your own—Jesus is your source of strength, and through Him, you can do all things. Embrace the truth that in Christ, you already have victory over every weakness, and He will continue to strengthen you for the journey ahead.

Reflect

How has Christ's strength carried you through weak moments in your life? How can you continue to rely on His strength in the future?

Week 2: Standing Firm in the Lord

In a world full of uncertainty, challenges, and temptations, standing firm in the Lord is essential for a life of faith. When we build our foundation on Christ, we can withstand the storms that life brings. This week will focus on learning to stand firm in God's truth, holding on to faith in difficult times, and being anchored in His promises. Through His strength, we can remain steadfast no matter what we face.

October 8

Building Your Life on Christ

"Therefore everyone who hears these words of mine and puts them into practice is like a wise man who built his house on the rock."
Matthew 7:24

The foundation of your faith is critical for standing firm. Jesus is the solid rock on which we can build our lives. When we root ourselves in Him, we are able to withstand the trials and pressures of life. This week, take time to reflect on the foundation of your life. Are you building on Christ, or on things that can be shaken?

Reflect

In what areas of your life do you need to rebuild your foundation on Christ? How can you make Him your anchor during difficult times?

October 9

Holding on to Faith in the Storms

"Let us hold unswervingly to the hope we profess, for He who promised is faithful."
Hebrews 10:23

Life often brings unexpected storms—health issues, financial struggles, broken relationships—but our faith in God is what keeps us grounded. Standing firm means clinging to the hope we have in Christ, even when circumstances are tough. This week, focus on holding onto your faith, knowing that God is faithful and His promises will never fail.

Prayer

Lord, help me to hold on to my faith in You when life gets difficult. Strengthen me to trust in Your faithfulness and never lose sight of Your promises.

October 10

Standing Strong Against Temptation

"Be on your guard; stand firm in the faith; be courageous; be strong."

1 Corinthians 16:13

Temptation is inevitable, but through God's strength, we can resist and stand firm in our faith. Whether it's the temptation to give in to doubt, fear, or sin, standing strong means recognizing the traps of the enemy and choosing to follow God's path. This week, focus on identifying areas of temptation in your life and ask God for the courage and strength to stand firm against them.

Reflect

Where do you feel most tempted to stray from your faith? How can you seek God's strength to overcome those temptations?

October 11

Anchored in God's Word

"Your word is a lamp for my feet, a light on my path."

Psalm 119:105

God's Word is essential for standing firm in faith. It guides us, encourages us, and reminds us of His truth when the world offers conflicting messages. This week, make God's Word your anchor. As you study Scripture, allow it to strengthen you and give you the confidence to stand firm in the face of challenges.

Prayer

Lord, help me to stand firm in Your Word. Let it be the foundation of my life, guiding me in truth and keeping me steady through every circumstance.

October 12

Standing Firm Through Prayer

"Devote yourselves to prayer, being watchful and thankful."
Colossians 4:2

Prayer is a powerful tool for standing firm in the Lord. Through prayer, we stay connected to God, receive His wisdom, and find the strength to persevere. This week, make prayer a priority. Commit to spending time with God daily, asking for His guidance, and trusting Him to give you the strength to remain steadfast in your faith.

Reflect

How is your prayer life currently? In what ways can you deepen your connection with God through prayer so that you can stand firm in your faith?

October 13

Encouraging One Another to Stand Firm

"Therefore encourage one another and build each other up, just as in fact you are d
1 Thessalonians 5:11

Standing firm isn't something we do alone. God calls us to be in community, encouraging one another and helping each other to stay strong in faith. This week, take time to encourage those around you in their walk with the Lord. Offer prayer, words of encouragement, or practical support to help others stand firm in their faith.

Reflect

Who in your life needs encouragement to stand firm in their faith? How can you be a source of support and strength to those around you?

October 14

Finding Strength in God's Faithfulness

"The Lord is faithful, and He will strengthen you and protect you from the evil one."
2 Thessalonians 3:3

As you conclude this week, reflect on God's faithfulness. He is the source of your strength and protection. When we feel weak or vulnerable, it's His faithfulness that keeps us standing firm. Trust that no matter what comes your way, God will continue to uphold you with His strength.

Prayer

Lord, thank You for Your faithfulness. Help me to stand firm in You, trusting that You will continue to strengthen me and protect me as I walk with You.

Week 3: God's Strength in Your Weakness

One of the greatest mysteries of faith is how God's strength is most evident in our moments of weakness. When we reach the end of our abilities, resources, or understanding, that's when God steps in with His limitless power. This week, we will explore the beauty of God's strength made perfect in our weaknesses, and how we can experience His power in every area of our lives where we feel lacking.

October 15

Embracing Your Weakness

"But He said to me, 'My grace is sufficient for you, for My power is made perfect in weakness.' Therefore I will boast all the more gladly about my weaknesses, so that Christ's power may rest on me."
2 Corinthians 12:9

We often think of weakness as something to hide or overcome. But the apostle Paul teaches us a different perspective—boasting in our weaknesses so that Christ's power can rest on us. This day, reflect on your own areas of weakness and instead of hiding them, embrace them as an opportunity for God's strength to be displayed.

Reflect

What weaknesses have you been hiding or avoiding? How can you invite God to work through them?

October 16

Surrendering to God's Power

"I can do all this through Him who gives me strength."
Philippians 4:13

Strength doesn't come from self-reliance but from complete dependence on God. We are often tempted to try to do things in our own power, but true strength is found when we surrender to God and allow Him to work in and through us. Today, practice letting go of self-sufficiency and lean on

God for your strength.

Prayer

Lord, I surrender my desire to control things and do them in my own strength. Teach me to rely on Your power in every area of my life.

October 17

Finding God's Strength in Times of Trial

"The Lord is my strength and my shield; my heart trusts in Him, and He helps me. My heart leaps for joy, and with my song I praise Him."

Psalm 28:7

Trials have a way of revealing our limitations. When we face adversity, it can be easy to feel weak, but these are the moments when God's strength becomes most evident. This day, consider the trials you are facing and trust that God is your strength and shield, ready to carry you through.

Reflect

In what trials are you currently seeking God's strength? How has He been your shield during difficult moments in the past?

October 18

Strengthened by His Grace

"You then, my son, be strong in the grace that is in Christ Jesus."

2 Timothy 2:1

God's grace not only saves us but strengthens us for the journey. His grace is sufficient for every challenge and every season of life. No matter how inadequate or weak you may feel, God's grace is more than enough. Today, ask God to strengthen you through His grace, knowing that His favor rests on you.

Prayer

Lord, thank You for Your grace that strengthens me each day. Help me to trust that Your grace is enough, even in my moments of weakness.

October 19

Persevering in Weakness

"Consider it pure joy, my brothers and sisters, whenever you face trials of many kinds, because you know that the testing of your faith produces perseverance."

James 1:2-3

When we experience weakness, it can be tempting to give up or lose heart. But God uses these moments to build perseverance in us. He strengthens us not by removing the weakness but by helping us endure and grow through it. Today, focus on how God is using your current challenges to build perseverance and strengthen your faith.

Reflect

What trials have tested your faith recently? How can you embrace those moments as opportunities for spiritual growth?

October 20

The Power of Humility

"Humble yourselves before the Lord, and He will lift you up."

James 4:10

Humility is the key to experiencing God's strength in our weakness. When we humble ourselves and acknowledge our need for God, He lifts us up. This day, practice humility by recognizing areas where you've been relying on your own strength and ask God to fill those places with His power.

Prayer

Lord, I humble myself before You. I acknowledge that I can't do it all on my own. Please lift me up with Your strength and help me trust in Your power rather than my own.

October 21

Strength for Every Season

"Even youths grow tired and weary, and young men stumble and fall; but those who hope in the Lord will renew their strength. They will soar on wings like eagles; they will run and not grow weary, they will walk and not be faint."

Isaiah 40:30-31

God promises to renew the strength of those who hope in Him. No matter the season of life or the challenges you face, God is faithful to provide the strength you need. As you end this week, place your hope in the Lord and trust that He will continue to renew your strength, allowing you to soar even in difficult times.

Reflect

How has God renewed your strength in past seasons of life? How can you continue to place your hope in Him for the strength you need?

Week 4: Finding Rest in His Strength

Rest is a gift from God, yet it can be hard to fully embrace it in a world that celebrates constant busyness and self-reliance. But when we lean on God's strength instead of our own, we discover a deeper, more enduring kind of rest—one that refreshes our souls and renews our spirits. This week, we will explore what it means to rest in God's strength, trusting that His power is enough for every area of our lives.

October 22

Rest for the Weary

"Come to me, all you who are weary and burdened, and I will give you rest."

Matthew 11:28

Jesus invites the weary to come to Him and find rest. He knows the weight we carry and understands our need for relief. This rest isn't just physical but spiritual and emotional. Today, reflect on the areas where you feel weary and heavy-laden. Jesus is inviting you to release those burdens and rest in His strength.

Prayer

Lord, I come to You with the burdens that weigh me down. Teach me to rest in Your strength and find peace in Your presence.

October 23

Trusting in God's Timing

"Be still before the Lord and wait patiently for Him."

Psalm 37:7

Resting in God's strength also means trusting His timing. When we try to force things to happen in our own way or on our schedule, we exhaust ourselves. But when we wait on the Lord, trusting that His plans and timing are perfect, we find peace. This day, take time to be still before God, trusting that He is working in ways you cannot yet see.

Reflect

Where in your life are you struggling to wait on God's timing? How can you practice stillness and trust in Him today?

October 24

Resting in God's Care

"Cast all your anxiety on Him because He cares for you."
1 Peter 5:7

God cares deeply for you, and He invites you to cast all your worries and anxieties onto Him. Resting in His strength means letting go of your cares and trusting that He is taking care of everything. Today, make it a practice to give your worries over to God, knowing that His strength is sufficient to carry them.

Prayer

Father, I give You my anxieties and worries. Help me to trust in Your care and rest in the knowledge that You are in control.

October 25

Resting in God's Grace

"But those who hope in the Lord will renew their strength."
Isaiah 40:31

When we rely on our own efforts, we quickly become drained. But when we place our hope in the Lord, He renews our strength. This renewal comes from resting in God's grace, knowing that we don't have to earn His favor or try harder to please Him. Today, rest in the truth that God's grace is sufficient, and let Him renew your strength as you trust in

Him.

Reflect

How have you been trying to earn God's favor or rely on your own strength? What would it look like to rest in His grace instead?

October 26

The Sabbath Rest

"Remember the Sabbath day by keeping it holy."
Exodus 20:8

God designed the Sabbath as a day of rest, not just to cease from work, but to restore our souls by reconnecting with Him. Observing a Sabbath rest is an act of trust—trusting that God will provide for our needs and that we can stop striving. This day, reflect on how you can incorporate Sabbath rest into your life, not just as a day but as a rhythm of trusting God throughout your week.

Reflect

How can you intentionally incorporate Sabbath rest into your routine? What areas of your life need rest and restoration?

October 27

Finding Rest in God's Presence

"My presence will go with you, and I will give you rest."
Exodus 33:14

God promises His presence will go with us, giving us rest. There is a peace that comes when we spend time in God's presence, laying aside the noise and distractions of life to simply be with Him. Today, set aside time to sit in God's presence, allowing His peace to calm your heart and mind.

Prayer

Lord, I desire to rest in Your presence. Quiet the noise of the world around me and let me find peace in You today.

October 28

Living from a Place of Rest

"In repentance and rest is your salvation, in quietness and trust is your strength."

Isaiah 30:15

Rest is not just a momentary pause; it is a way of life when we live from a place of quiet trust in God. True strength comes from resting in Him daily, trusting that His power is at work in our lives even when we can't see it. As you conclude this week, focus on making rest in God's strength a continual practice, knowing that His grace, love, and power are more than enough.

Reflect

How can you live from a place of rest and trust in God, rather than striving in your own strength? What changes can you make to create space for rest in your daily life?

11

November

Week 1: The Power of Thankfulness

Gratitude is a powerful force in the life of a believer. It shifts our perspective from focusing on what we lack to appreciating all that God has provided. A thankful heart not only draws us closer to God but also brings peace, joy, and contentment, even in difficult circumstances. This week, we will explore the transformative power of thankfulness and how it can strengthen our relationship with God and others.

November 1

Giving Thanks in All Circumstances

"Give thanks in all circumstances; for this is God's will for you in Christ Jesus."

1 Thessalonians 5:18

God calls us to give thanks in *all* circumstances, not just when things are going well. Gratitude in the face of challenges reflects our trust in God's goodness and sovereignty. Today, take a moment to thank God for His faithfulness, even in the difficult or uncertain situations in your life.

Reflect

In what areas of your life is it hard to give thanks? How can you shift your perspective to see God's hand at work in those situations?

November 2

The Peace that Comes from Gratitude

"Do not be anxious about anything, but in every situation, by prayer and petition, with thanksgiving, present your requests to God. And the peace of God, which transcends all understanding, will guard your hearts and your minds in Christ Jesus."
Philippians 4:6-7

When we bring our worries and concerns to God with a thankful heart, He exchanges our anxiety for His peace. Thanksgiving shifts our focus from our problems to God's ability to provide and sustain us. Today, instead of dwelling on what's worrying you, focus on the blessings God has already given, and let His peace guard your heart.

Prayer

Lord, thank You for Your provision and care. Help me to turn to You with a grateful heart and experience Your peace, even in the midst of life's challenges.

November 3

Gratitude as Worship

"Enter His gates with thanksgiving and His courts with praise; give thanks to Him and praise His name."

Psalm 100:4

Thankfulness is a form of worship. When we thank God for who He is and all He has done, we are glorifying Him and expressing our trust in His goodness. Today, spend time in worship, thanking God for His faithfulness, His grace, and His presence in your life.

Reflect

What specific things can you thank God for today? How can you make gratitude a regular part of your worship?

November 4

Gratitude in Times of Waiting

"Wait for the Lord; be strong and take heart and wait for the Lord."

Psalm 27:14

Waiting can be one of the hardest parts of life, but even in waiting, we can give thanks. Gratitude during waiting seasons demonstrates trust in God's perfect timing and His plans for our good. Today, if you find yourself in a season of waiting, thank God for what He is doing behind the scenes, and trust that His timing is best.

Prayer

Father, help me to trust You in the waiting. Thank You for the ways You are working, even when I can't see it. Strengthen my faith as I wait for Your perfect timing.

November 5

Cultivating a Thankful Heart

"Let the peace of Christ rule in your hearts, since as members of one body you were called to peace. And be thankful."

Colossians 3:15

A thankful heart doesn't come naturally—it's something we cultivate over time by intentionally focusing on God's goodness. Today, start a gratitude journal, listing at least three things you are thankful for each day. As you cultivate thankfulness, you will notice how it transforms your attitude and strengthens your faith.

Reflect

How can you make thankfulness a daily habit? What small practices can you implement to cultivate a grateful heart in your everyday life?

November 6

Thankfulness in Relationships

"I thank my God every time I remember you."
Philippians 1:3

Thankfulness not only impacts our relationship with God but also our relationships with others. Gratitude for the people in our lives fosters love, encouragement, and unity. Today, take a moment to thank God for the important people in your life, and consider expressing your gratitude to them in a tangible way.

Reflect

Who in your life are you thankful for today? How can you express that thankfulness in a meaningful way?

November 7

The Overflow of Gratitude

"Give thanks to the Lord, for He is good; His love endures forever."

Psalm 107:1

Gratitude has a ripple effect. As we cultivate thankfulness in our hearts, it overflows into every aspect of our lives, blessing others and reflecting God's goodness to the world. As you close this week, reflect on how you can live a life that overflows with gratitude, making thankfulness not just an occasional act, but a way of life.

Prayer

Lord, thank You for Your unending goodness and love. Help me to live with a heart that overflows with gratitude, so that others may see Your goodness through me.

Week 2: Being Content in Every Circumstance

Contentment is not based on what we have or our external circumstances but on the deep trust that God is enough for us. In a world that constantly pushes us to seek more, contentment can feel elusive. Yet, the apostle Paul teaches us that contentment is learned and comes from knowing Christ and relying on His strength. This week, we will dive into what it means to find true contentment, no matter what we face, and how to rest in God's provision and sufficiency.

November 8

Learning the Secret of Contentment

"I have learned to be content whatever the circumstances. I know what it is to be in need, and I know what it is to have plenty. I have learned the secret of being content in any and every situation, whether well-fed or hungry, whether living in plenty or in want. I

can do all this through Him who gives me strength."
Philippians 4:11-13

Paul's secret to contentment was not dependent on his situation but on Christ. He knew that whether he had little or much, Christ was his source of strength and peace. Today, reflect on how your contentment is affected by your circumstances. What would it look like to find contentment through Christ alone?

Reflect

In what areas of your life are you struggling to feel content? How can you shift your focus from your circumstances to Christ's sufficiency?

November 9

Trusting in God's Provision

"And my God will meet all your needs according to the riches of His glory in Christ Jesus."
Philippians 4:19

Contentment is closely tied to trust. When we trust that God will provide for our needs, we can rest in His provision rather than striving for more. Today, focus on the ways God has faithfully provided for you in the past and trust that He will continue to meet your needs in the future.

Prayer

Lord, thank You for always providing for me. Help me to trust You fully and be content, knowing that You will meet all my needs according to Your riches.

November 10

Contentment and Gratitude

"But godliness with contentment is great gain. For we brought nothing into the world, and we can take nothing out of it. But if we have food and clothing, we will be content with that."

1 Timothy 6:6-8

When we focus on what we lack, we can miss the blessings God has already provided. Contentment grows when we pair it with gratitude. Today, take time to thank God for what you already have, no matter how small it may seem, and watch how it transforms your heart toward contentment.

Reflect

What are some simple things you can be grateful for today? How does expressing gratitude lead to a deeper sense of contentment?

November 11

Avoiding the Trap of Comparison

"Each one should test their own actions. Then they can take pride in themselves alone, without comparing themselves to someone else."

Galatians 6:4

Comparison is one of the greatest enemies of contentment. When we compare our lives, our possessions, or our status to others, we can quickly become dissatisfied with what God has given us. Today, make a conscious decision to stop comparing yourself to others and instead be grateful for your own unique journey.

Prayer

Lord, help me to stop comparing my life to others. Teach me

to focus on the blessings You have given me and to be content in the path You have set before me.

November 12

Finding Contentment in God's Presence

"The Lord is my shepherd, I lack nothing."

Psalm 23:1

True contentment comes from recognizing that when we have God, we truly lack nothing. His presence is enough to satisfy our deepest longings. Today, meditate on Psalm 23 and rest in the truth that with the Lord as your shepherd, you have everything you need.

Reflect

How does knowing that the Lord is your shepherd change your perspective on contentment? In what ways have you experienced God's provision and care?

November 13

Contentment in Difficult Times

"Keep your lives free from the love of money and be content with what you have, because God has said, 'Never will I leave you; never will I forsake you.'"

Hebrews 13:5

Even in difficult times, when we may feel that we lack security, resources, or comfort, we can find contentment in God's promise that He will never leave or forsake us. This day, reflect on how God's presence is your greatest source of contentment, even when your circumstances are less than ideal.

Prayer

Lord, even in hard times, I trust that You are with me. Help me to be content in Your constant presence and to rely on You instead of material things for my security.

November 14

Contentment Leads to Peace

"Peace I leave with you; My peace I give you. I do not give to you as the world gives. Do not let your hearts be troubled and do not be afraid."

John 14:27

When we find contentment in Christ, we experience a peace that the world cannot offer. This peace comes from knowing that God is in control, that He provides for our needs, and that His presence is enough. As you conclude this week, focus on resting in the peace that comes from contentment in God.

Reflect

How has cultivating contentment in Christ brought peace to your heart this week? How can you continue to nurture this contentment in your daily life?

Week 3: Recognizing God's Blessings

Recognizing God's blessings in our lives requires intentionality. In the hustle of everyday life, it's easy to overlook the countless ways God is providing, guiding, and blessing us. This week, we will focus on developing eyes to see God's hand at work and hearts that respond with gratitude. As we recognize His blessings, we grow in appreciation for His goodness and deepen our relationship with Him.

November 15

Every Good Gift is From God

"Every good and perfect gift is from above, coming down from the Father of the heavenly lights, who does not change like shifting shadows."

James 1:17

Everything good in your life, no matter how big or small, is a gift from God. When we begin to see all that we have as coming from His hand, our hearts are filled with gratitude and awe. Today, take time to reflect on the good things in your life—whether it's relationships, provisions, or moments of joy—and recognize them as gifts from your heavenly Father.

Reflect

What are some good and perfect gifts that God has given you recently? How does viewing them as gifts from God change your perspective?

November 16

God's Blessings in the Everyday

"Blessed be the Lord, who daily loads us with benefits, the God of our salvation!"

Psalm 68:19

God's blessings aren't just for big, life-changing moments; He blesses us daily with His goodness, care, and provision. Often, these blessings can be found in the mundane and routine parts of life. Today, as you go about your normal day, pay attention to the small blessings that God is placing before you.

Prayer

Lord, thank You for the daily blessings You give me. Help me to notice and appreciate the ways You are at work in my everyday life, even in the smallest details.

November 17

Blessings in Disguise

"And we know that in all things God works for the good of those who love Him, who have been called according to His purpose."

Romans 8:28

Sometimes God's blessings come in ways we don't expect—through difficult times, challenges, or unexpected detours. These "blessings in disguise" shape our character, draw us closer to God, and work for our ultimate good. Today, reflect on how God has brought blessings through hardship, and thank Him for working in all things for your good.

Reflect

Can you think of a time when a difficult situation eventually led to a blessing? How did that experience deepen your trust in God's plans for you?

November 18

Blessings in Relationships

"A friend loves at all times, and a brother is born for a time of adversity."

Proverbs 17:17

One of the greatest blessings God gives us is the gift of relationships—friends, family, and mentors who walk with us through life's journey. These people support, encourage, and challenge us, often being the hands and feet of Christ in our lives. Today, reflect on the relationships that have been a blessing to you and take a moment to express gratitude to God for them.

Prayer

Lord, thank You for the people You've placed in my life. Help me to recognize them as blessings from You and to cherish the relationships that reflect Your love and care.

November 19

Recognizing Spiritual Blessings

"Praise be to the God and Father of our Lord Jesus Christ, who has blessed us in the heavenly realms with every spiritual blessing in Christ."

Ephesians 1:3

While material blessings are wonderful, the greatest blessings we have are spiritual—our salvation, the indwelling of the Holy Spirit, and the promise of eternal life. Today, focus on the spiritual blessings you've received through Christ and thank God for the immeasurable richness of His grace.

Reflect

What spiritual blessings have you received in Christ? How can you celebrate these eternal gifts in your daily life?

November 20

Counting Your Blessings

"Let all that I am praise the Lord; may I never forget the good things He does for me."

Psalm 103:2

It's easy to take God's blessings for granted or to forget them when life gets busy or challenging. But when we take time to count our blessings, we remember God's faithfulness and His goodness. Today, make a list of the blessings you can recall from the past week, month, or year, and offer them to God in praise.

Prayer

Lord, I never want to forget the good things You've done for me. Help me to be mindful of Your blessings, and give me a heart of gratitude for all You have provided.

November 21

Blessing Others from Your Abundance

"You will be enriched in every way so that you can be generous on every occasion, and through us your generosity will result in thanksgiving to God."

2 Corinthians 9:11

God blesses us not only for our own benefit but also so we can be a blessing to others. As you conclude this week, reflect on how you can share the blessings God has given you—whether they are material, emotional, or spiritual—with those around you. In doing so, you will bring glory to God and spread His love to others.

Reflect

How has God blessed you in a way that you can share with others? What steps can you take this week to be a blessing to someone else?

Week 4: Gratitude as a Spiritual Practice

Gratitude is more than a reaction to receiving good things; it's a spiritual discipline that draws us closer to God and transforms our perspective. When we practice gratitude regularly, we begin to see God's hand at work in all circumstances, cultivating a heart of thankfulness that fuels our faith. This week, we will explore how gratitude can become a key part of our spiritual walk, helping us grow in our relationship with God and live with a deep sense of peace and joy.

November 22

Gratitude in All Circumstances

"Give thanks in all circumstances; for this is God's will for you in Christ Jesus."

1 Thessalonians 5:18

God calls us to give thanks in every situation, not just when things are going well. Gratitude, even in difficult times, is an act of trust that acknowledges God's sovereignty and goodness. Today, think of a challenging circumstance you are facing and take a moment to thank God for His presence with you, trusting that He is working through it for your good.

Reflect

How can you cultivate gratitude even in hard situations? What impact does this have on your faith?

November 23

Gratitude Draws Us Closer to God

"Enter His gates with thanksgiving and His courts with praise; give thanks to Him and praise His name."

Psalm 100:4

Gratitude opens the door for a deeper connection with God. When we approach God with thankfulness, we acknowledge His goodness and draw nearer to His presence. Today, spend time in prayer and focus on thanking God for who He is, beyond just the blessings you've received.

Prayer

Lord, thank You for who You are—for Your love, Your faithfulness, and Your grace. Help me to approach You daily with a heart full of gratitude, recognizing that every good thing comes from You.

November 24

Gratitude as a Form of Worship

"I will give thanks to the Lord with my whole heart; I will recount all of Your wonderful deeds."

Psalm 9:1

Gratitude is a powerful form of worship. When we take time to thank God, we honor Him and give Him the glory for the good things He has done. Today, reflect on the past few months and make a list of the ways God has worked in your life. Offer this list to Him as an act of worship, praising Him for His faithfulness.

Reflect

How has gratitude enhanced your worship of God? What are some specific ways you can express gratitude as part of your daily worship?

November 25

Gratitude Changes Our Perspective

"And let the peace of Christ rule in your hearts, to which indeed you were called in one body. And be thankful."
Colossians 3:15

When we practice gratitude, we shift our focus from what is lacking to what we have already received. This shift in perspective leads to greater peace and contentment, as we become more aware of God's provision in our lives. Today, reflect on how a spirit of thankfulness can bring peace to areas where you may feel anxious or unsatisfied.

Prayer

Lord, help me to see my life through the lens of gratitude. Shift my focus from what I don't have to what You have already provided. Let Your peace rule in my heart as I thank You for Your faithfulness.

November 26

Gratitude Leads to Joy

"The Lord has done great things for us, and we are filled with joy."
Psalm 126:3

Gratitude naturally leads to joy because it reminds us of the goodness of God and the blessings He has poured into our lives. When we choose to focus on God's blessings, no matter our circumstances, joy follows. Today, take time to intentionally thank God for specific blessings and notice how your heart responds with joy.

Reflect

How does gratitude lead to a deeper sense of joy in your life? What are some ways you can practice thankfulness to experience more of God's joy?

November 27

Gratitude in Prayer

"Do not be anxious about anything, but in every situation, by prayer and petition, with thanksgiving, present your requests to God."

Philippians 4:6

Gratitude is an important part of our prayer life. When we combine our requests with thanksgiving, we approach God with a heart that acknowledges His past faithfulness and trusts in His future provision. Today, as you bring your needs to God, remember to include thanksgiving for how He has already answered prayers in the past.

Prayer

Lord, as I bring my needs before You, I also want to thank You for all the ways You have been faithful in my life. Help me to pray with a heart full of gratitude, trusting in Your goodness.

November 28

Gratitude as a Daily Practice

"Bless the Lord, O my soul, and forget not all His benefits."

Psalm 103:2

Gratitude should be a daily practice, not just something we express on special occasions. When we regularly take time to thank God, we nurture a heart that is more in tune with His presence and His blessings. As you conclude this week, commit to making gratitude a part of your daily routine, whether through prayer, journaling, or simply pausing to give thanks throughout your day.

Reflect

How can you make gratitude a consistent practice in your life? What tools or habits can help you cultivate a spirit of thankfulness each day?

12

December

Week 1: The Hope of the Gospel

The gospel—the good news of Jesus Christ—offers hope that transcends circumstances, pain, and uncertainty. Through the gospel, we find not only the promise of eternal life but also the assurance of God's love, grace, and redemption in every moment of our lives. This week, we will explore the transformative power of the gospel and how it fills us with hope in all situations.

December 1

The Good News of Jesus

"For God so loved the world that He gave His one and only Son, that whoever believes in Him shall not perish but have eternal life."
John 3:16

The foundation of our hope is found in the simple yet profound truth that God loves us so deeply that He sent His Son to save us. This gift of salvation is the ultimate source of hope, giving us confidence in God's love and our eternal future with Him. Today, take a moment to reflect on the power of the gospel and how it has changed your life.

Reflect

How has the good news of Jesus given you hope? How can you share this hope with others?

December 2

The Assurance of Salvation

"I write these things to you who believe in the name of the Son of God so that you may know that you have eternal life.

1 John 5:13

The hope of the gospel includes the assurance that, through Christ, we have eternal life. This is not a hope based on uncertainty, but a confident expectation grounded in God's promises. Today, rest in the assurance of your salvation and let it fill your heart with peace and hope.

Prayer

Lord, thank You for the assurance of eternal life through Your Son. Help me to live each day with the confident hope that comes from knowing I am secure in Your love and grace.

December 3

Hope in Times of Suffering

"Not only so, but we also glory in our sufferings, because we know that suffering produces perseverance; perseverance, character; and character, hope."

Romans 5:3-4

Even in times of suffering, the gospel gives us hope. Through our pain and trials, God is at work, building our character and deepening our faith. The hope we have in Christ enables us to endure difficult seasons, knowing that He is using them for our good and His glory. Today, reflect on how the gospel brings hope in your own times of suffering.

Reflect

How has the hope of the gospel sustained you during difficult times? What can you learn from those experiences?

December 4

The Hope of Redemption

"He has rescued us from the dominion of darkness and brought us into the kingdom of the Son He loves, in whom we have redemption, the forgiveness of sins."
Colossians 1:13-14

The gospel is the story of God's redemptive work, not just for our eternal future but for our daily lives. Through Christ, we are rescued from sin, shame, and darkness, and brought into the light of God's kingdom. This redemption offers hope that no matter where we've been, God is always at work restoring us. Today, embrace the hope that comes from knowing you are redeemed.

Prayer

Lord, thank You for rescuing me from darkness and bringing me into Your kingdom. Help me to live in the hope of redemption, trusting that You are continually at work in my life.

December 5

Living in the Hope of the Gospel

"Praise be to the God and Father of our Lord Jesus Christ! In His great mercy, He has given us new birth into a living hope through the resurrection of Jesus Christ from the dead."

1 Peter 1:3

The hope of the gospel is a "living hope"—one that sustains and empowers us in our daily lives. Because of Christ's resurrection, we have hope not only for the future but for the present. This living hope gives us strength to face challenges, courage to walk in faith, and joy to serve others. Today, reflect on how the gospel brings hope into your everyday life.

Reflect

How can you live out the hope of the gospel in your daily actions? In what areas of your life do you need to embrace this living hope more fully?

December 6

Sharing the Hope of the Gospel

"But in your hearts revere Christ as Lord. Always be prepared to give an answer to everyone who asks you to give the reason for the hope that you have."

1 Peter 3:15

The hope we have in Christ is not meant to be kept to ourselves—it is a hope that should overflow and be shared with others. As we live in the joy and confidence of the gospel, others will notice and may ask about the hope that sets us apart. Today, consider how you can share the hope of the gospel with someone in your life.

Prayer

Lord, help me to live in such a way that others see the hope of the gospel in me. Give me the words and courage to share this hope with those around me, pointing them to Your love and salvation.

December 7

Hope in Christ's Return

"While we wait for the blessed hope—the appearing of the glory of our great God and Savior, Jesus Christ."

Titus 2:13

Our ultimate hope as Christians is the return of Christ, when He will make all things new and restore creation to its intended glory. This "blessed hope" gives us confidence as we wait for the day when God's kingdom will come in fullness. Today, reflect on the hope of Christ's return and how it shapes your perspective on life.

Reflect

How does the promise of Christ's return give you hope in the present? How can you live with an eternal perspective, trusting in the fulfillment of God's promises?

Week 2: Finding Hope in Dark Times

Life can bring seasons of darkness that challenge our faith and test our endurance. Yet, even in these times, God's light can break through, offering hope and strength when we feel weak. The Bible is filled with reminders that God is close to the brokenhearted and offers a hope that is unshakeable, even in the midst of our pain. This week, we will explore how to hold onto hope when facing life's darkest moments and find God's presence in our struggles.

December 8

God is Near to the Brokenhearted

"The Lord is close to the brokenhearted and saves those who are crushed in spirit."

Psalm 34:18

When we are hurting, God draws near to us in a special way. He sees our pain, hears our cries, and holds us close. No matter how alone we may feel, we can find comfort in knowing that God is always with us in our brokenness. Today, take a moment to rest in His presence, knowing that He is near and cares deeply for you.

Reflect

How does knowing that God is close to the brokenhearted bring you comfort? In what ways can you invite His presence into your pain?

December 9

Hope in God's Promises

"For I know the plans I have for you," declares the Lord, "plans to prosper you and not to harm you, plans to give you hope and a future."

Jeremiah 29:11

God's promises provide a foundation of hope, even when our circumstances feel uncertain or discouraging. He has good plans for us, filled with hope and purpose, even if we cannot see them fully yet. Today, reflect on God's promises in your life and hold onto them as anchors of hope in difficult times.

Prayer

Lord, thank You for Your promises and the hope they give me. Help me to trust in Your plans, even when I cannot see the path ahead.

December 10

Finding Strength in Weakness

"But He said to me, 'My grace is sufficient for you, for My power is made perfect in weakness.' Therefore I will boast all the more gladly about my weaknesses, so that Christ's power may rest on me."

2 Corinthians 12:9

In our weakest moments, God's strength shines through. When we feel unable to carry on, we can rely on His grace to sustain us. The hope of the gospel is that God's strength is made perfect in our weakness, allowing us to rest in His power. Today, lean on God's strength and let Him be your source of endurance.

Reflect

How can you lean on God's strength when you feel weak? What does it mean to you that His grace is sufficient for every struggle?

December 11

Light in the Darkness

"The light shines in the darkness, and the darkness has not overcome it."

John 1:5

God's light shines brightest in our darkest moments, reminding us that nothing can extinguish His hope. No matter how difficult our circumstances, we can hold onto the truth that His light will always overcome the darkness. Today, ask God to shine His light into any area of your life that feels dark or heavy, trusting that He is with you.

Prayer

Lord, thank You that Your light is stronger than any darkness. Help me to see Your presence in my life and to trust that You are with me, even in my darkest moments.

December 12

Choosing to Hope in God's Faithfulness

"Yet this I call to mind and therefore I have hope: Because of the Lord's great love we are not consumed, for His compassions never fail. They are new every morning; great is Your faithfulness."
Lamentations 3:21-23

Even when life feels overwhelming, we can choose to hope in God's unchanging faithfulness. His love, compassion, and mercy are new each day, providing fresh strength and comfort. Today, remember God's faithfulness in your life and let it renew your hope.

Reflect

How can you remind yourself of God's faithfulness when you feel hopeless? What are some ways you have seen His compassion in your life?

December 13

Endurance Through Hope

"But those who hope in the Lord will renew their strength. They will soar on wings like eagles; they will run and not grow weary,

they will walk and not be faint."
Isaiah 40:31

Hoping in God gives us the strength to endure, even when we feel like giving up. His strength sustains us, lifting us above our struggles and renewing our spirits. Today, bring your burdens to God and ask Him to fill you with fresh strength and perseverance.

Prayer

Lord, thank You for the strength that comes from hoping in You. Renew my spirit today and help me to endure with faith, knowing that You are carrying me through.

December 14

Hope Beyond Circumstances

"We have this hope as an anchor for the soul, firm and secure."
Hebrews 6:19

Our hope in God is not dependent on circumstances; it is an anchor that holds us steady, even when life feels turbulent. This hope is secure because it is grounded in God's promises and character. Today, reflect on how God's hope has been an anchor for your soul and how you can cling to it in challenging times.

Reflect

How has hope in God anchored you during difficult seasons? What steps can you take to hold onto this hope more firmly in your daily life?

Week 3: Hope for the Future

God promises us a future filled with hope, where He holds every detail and purpose in His hands. Even when the road ahead seems uncertain, we can trust that He is working everything for our good. This week, we will focus on trusting God with our future, learning to release control, and embracing the peace that comes from placing our hope in His perfect plan.

December 15

Trusting God with Tomorrow

"Therefore do not worry about tomorrow, for tomorrow will worry about itself. Each day has enough trouble of its own.

Matthew 6:34

Jesus reminds us not to worry about the future, as God cares for every need we have. By placing our trust in Him, we free ourselves from the anxieties that can arise when we try to control what lies ahead. Today, release any worries you have about the future and trust that God has tomorrow in His hands.

Reflect

What future concerns are weighing on your heart? How can you hand them over to God today, trusting Him to provide?

December 16

God's Plan is Perfect

"For I know the plans I have for you," declares the Lord, "plans to prosper you and not to harm you, plans to give you hope and a future."

Jeremiah 29:11

God's plans are always for our good, even when we cannot see how everything fits together. He holds our lives in His hands and desires to guide us toward a hopeful future. Today, remind yourself that God's plan is perfect and let go of any desire to control or understand every step of the journey.

Prayer

Lord, thank You for the plans You have for me. Help me to trust in Your purpose for my life and to release my need to understand everything along the way.

December 17

Hope in God's Timing

"He has made everything beautiful in its time."

Ecclesiastes 3:11

God's timing is often different from ours, but it is always perfect. He sees the bigger picture and knows exactly when things should unfold. While waiting for His plans to come to pass, we can trust that His timing is part of His loving provision for us. Today, let go of any frustration with the timing of your dreams and rest in the knowledge that God's timing is beautiful.

Reflect

Are there areas in your life where you are struggling with God's timing? How can you practice patience and trust in His perfect timing?

December 18

God's Faithfulness Through Generations

"But from everlasting to everlasting the Lord's love is with those who fear Him, and His righteousness with their children's

children."
Psalm 103:17

God's faithfulness extends beyond our lives to future generations. The hope we have in Him is an inheritance for those who come after us. Today, reflect on God's faithfulness throughout history and in your own life, knowing that He will continue to be faithful for generations to come.

Prayer

Lord, thank You for Your faithfulness to me and to all who have come before me. Help me to live in a way that leaves a legacy of hope and trust in You for those who follow.

December 19

God's Provision for Our Future

"And my God will meet all your needs according to the riches of His glory in Christ Jesus."
Philippians 4:19

God knows exactly what we need and promises to provide for us according to His abundant riches. Even when the future seems uncertain, we can have confidence that He will supply all our needs. Today, bring your hopes and needs for the future to God and trust Him to meet each one.

Reflect

How has God provided for you in the past? How does remembering His provision give you hope for the future?

December 20

Hope Beyond Earthly Life

"But our citizenship is in heaven. And we eagerly await a Savior

from there, the Lord Jesus Christ."
Philippians 3:20

As Christians, we look forward to an eternal hope that goes beyond this life. Knowing that our ultimate future is secure in Christ gives us strength and perspective in our earthly journey. Today, remind yourself that your true home is with God and let this hope give you peace and purpose as you look to the future.

Prayer

Lord, thank You for the promise of eternal life. Help me to live with an eternal perspective, holding onto the hope that my future with You is secure.

December 21

Embracing Hope for Today and Tomorrow

"May the God of hope fill you with all joy and peace as you trust in Him, so that you may overflow with hope by the power of the Holy Spirit."
Romans 15:13

God's hope is not just for tomorrow; it's for today as well. As we trust Him with our future, He fills us with joy and peace that overflow into every area of our lives. Today, invite the Holy Spirit to fill you with renewed hope for both today and tomorrow, trusting that God is guiding you every step of the way.

Reflect

How can you let go of any fears about the future and embrace God's hope for both today and tomorrow?

Week 4: Hope Renewed Through Christ's Coming

The promise of Christ's return is the foundation of our Christian hope. It reminds us that God is bringing about a future where all will be made right, and we will experience eternal joy in His presence. This week, we will focus on how the assurance of Christ's coming renews our hope each day, strengthens our faith, and calls us to live with anticipation and purpose.

Day 1: The Promise of Christ's Return

"And if I go and prepare a place for you, I will come back and take you to be with Me that you also may be where I am." — John 14:3 (NIV)

Jesus promises to return and take us to be with Him forever. This is our ultimate hope — that we will be with our Savior in a place He has prepared for us. Today, take time to reflect on the beauty of this promise and allow it to fill your heart with joy and expectation.

Reflection: How does the promise of Christ's return impact the way you view your daily life? What hope does it bring to you in times of struggle?

Day 2: Living with Expectation

"So you also must be ready, because the Son of Man will come at an hour when you do not expect Him." — Matthew 24:44 (NIV)

Christ calls us to live in readiness, watching for His return with anticipation. This expectation isn't just about waiting passively; it's an active hope that shapes our choices, values, and priorities. Today, consider what it means to live with an expectant heart and to align your life with the hope of His return.

Prayer: Lord, help me to live each day with a heart full of expectation, eagerly awaiting Your return and seeking to live in a way that honors You.

Day 3: Finding Strength in Our Eternal Hope

"For the grace of God has appeared that offers salvation to all people. It teaches us to say 'No' to ungodliness and worldly passions, and to live self-controlled, upright, and godly lives in this present age, while we wait for the blessed hope—the appearing of the glory of our great God and Savior, Jesus Christ." — Titus 2:11-13 (NIV)

Our hope in Christ's return gives us strength to live godly lives in the present. This "blessed hope" empowers us to resist the pull of the world and to focus on what truly matters. Today, draw strength from this hope and let it guide your actions, knowing that you are preparing for something greater than this world.

Reflection: How does your eternal hope help you stay focused on God's purposes? In what ways can you say "Yes" to God's ways and "No" to distractions?

Day 4: A New Heaven and a New Earth

"Then I saw 'a new heaven and a new earth,' for the first heaven and the first earth had passed away... He will wipe every tear from their eyes. There will be no more death or mourning or crying or pain, for the old order of things has passed away." — Revelation 21:1, 4 (NIV)

Our hope in Christ includes the promise of a restored creation, free from pain, death, and sorrow. This future fills us with hope that one day all brokenness will be healed. Today, meditate on this vision of a new heaven and earth, and allow it to renew your perspective and your hope.

Prayer: Lord, thank You for the promise of a restored world where pain and suffering will be no more. Help me to hold onto this hope and to look forward with joy to Your coming.

Day 5: Spreading the Hope of His Coming

"Therefore, encourage one another and build each other up, just as in fact you are doing." — 1 Thessalonians 5:11 (NIV)

Our hope in Christ's return is not something we keep to ourselves; it's a hope we are called to share and encourage others with. When we share this hope, we remind each other that our struggles are temporary and that eternal joy awaits. Today, reach out to someone who needs encouragement and share the hope of Christ with them.

Reflection: How can you encourage others with the hope of Christ's return? In what ways can you help others see the joy that lies ahead?

Day 6: Staying Faithful Until His Return

"Blessed is the one who perseveres under trial because, having stood the test, that person will receive the crown of life that the Lord has promised to those who love Him." —James 1:12 (NIV)

Christ's return calls us to live with perseverance and faithfulness, holding fast even when life is challenging. The promise of the "crown of life" is a reward that awaits those who stay faithful until the end. Today, let this hope give you strength to remain steadfast in your faith.

Prayer: Lord, thank You for the promise of eternal life. Help me to stay faithful, trusting that every trial I endure brings me closer to the joy of being with You forever.

Day 7: Living in Light of Eternity

"But our citizenship is in heaven. And we eagerly await a Savior from there, the Lord Jesus Christ." — Philippians 3:20 (NIV)

As citizens of heaven, we live with an eternal perspective, knowing that our true home is with Christ. This mindset shifts our priorities and keeps us focused on what truly matters. Today, renew your hope in the future and choose to live in a way that reflects the joy and peace of your heavenly citizenship.

Reflection: How does knowing that your home is in heaven influence your daily choices? In what ways can you live today in light of the eternity you eagerly await?

13

Special Devotions

Mother's Day: A Heart for Motherhood

Motherhood is a beautiful and sacred calling, one filled with sacrifice, strength, and boundless love. On Mother's Day, we celebrate the women who embrace this role with open hearts, sharing God's love through their nurturing, teaching, and care. Whether a biological mother, a stepmom, an adoptive mom, a grandmother, or a spiritual mother, each carries a unique expression of God's heart for His children. This devotion is a reflection on the virtues of motherhood and how they inspire us to see and share God's love.

Love That Knows No Bounds

"As a mother comforts her child, so will I comfort you."
Isaiah 66:13

A mother's love is perhaps the closest reflection we have of God's unconditional love. Just as God loves us without end, mothers give selflessly, comforting, nurturing, and sacrificing for the wellbeing of their children. On Mother's Day, we celebrate this incredible love and remember that God, too, holds us in His comforting embrace, surrounding us with His care.

Reflect

How does a mother's love remind you of God's love? Today, thank the mothers in your life for their constant care and for showing God's love through their own.

Prayer

Lord, thank You for mothers who reflect Your unfailing love. Help me to love others with the same grace, compassion, and selflessness.

Strength and Resilience in Every Season

"She is clothed with strength and dignity; she can laugh at the days to come."

Proverbs 31:25

Mothers are pillars of strength, enduring sleepless nights, carrying the burdens of their children, and standing firm in difficult times. This strength is a testament to God's sustaining power in their lives. Today, honor the strength of the mothers you know, remembering that they are a reflection of God's resilience and faithfulness.

Reflect

How can you show appreciation for the strength mothers bring to your life? Consider writing a note of gratitude to a mother who has demonstrated strength in your journey.

Prayer

Lord, thank You for giving mothers the strength to endure and persevere. May we be strengthened by their example and encouraged to stand firm in faith.

Wisdom and Guidance Rooted in Faith

"Start children off on the way they should go, and even when they are old they will not turn from it."
Proverbs 22:6

Mothers are teachers, shaping hearts and guiding their children in wisdom and truth. This role is a calling from God, who entrusts them to lead and guide with patience and grace. On Mother's Day, celebrate the wisdom that mothers impart, guiding us closer to God's path and helping us become who He has called us to be.

Reflect

What lessons have you learned from a mother in your life that have brought you closer to God? Consider sharing with her how she has impacted your walk of faith.

Prayer

Lord, thank You for the wisdom that mothers pass down. Help me to honor their guidance by walking faithfully in the path You have laid before me.

A Heart of Prayer and Intercession

"I prayed for this child, and the Lord has granted me what I asked of Him."
1 Samuel 1:27

Mothers often carry the gift of prayer, lifting up their children's needs before the Lord with faith and persistence. Like Hannah prayed for Samuel, mothers intercede on behalf of their children, seeking God's guidance and blessing in their lives.

Today, honor the prayers of mothers that have paved the way for blessings and breakthroughs.

Reflect

How has a mother's prayer affected your life? Take a moment to thank her for her faithfulness in prayer.

Prayer

Lord, thank You for the mothers who pray fervently for their children. May we be inspired by their devotion and bring all our needs to You in faith.

A Legacy of Faith and Love

"I am reminded of your sincere faith, which first lived in your grandmother Lois and in your mother Eunice and, I am persuaded, now lives in you also."

2 Timothy 1:5

A mother's faith has a lasting impact that echoes through generations, leaving a legacy of love and devotion to God. Paul's words to Timothy highlight this powerful legacy that mothers carry. On this Mother's Day, honor the faith that mothers pass down, a faith that impacts not only their own children but generations to come.

Reflect

What legacy of faith has a mother passed on to you? Think of ways you can honor and continue this legacy in your own life.

Prayer

Lord, thank You for the faithful mothers who have planted seeds of faith in our hearts. Help me to carry forward their legacy and pass it on to others.

14

Advent Devotionals: Preparing for Christ's Coming

Advent is a sacred time of anticipation and hope, a season dedicated to preparing our hearts to receive the light of Christ. Traditionally observed in the four weeks leading up to Christmas, Advent encourages us to pause, reflect, and make room for Jesus amid the busyness of holiday preparations. During these special Advent devotionals, we will meditate on themes of hope, peace, joy, and love—the pillars of the Advent season that bring our focus back to the meaning of Christmas.

These reflections will help you connect with the anticipation of God's people in Scripture, who awaited the Messiah with longing and faith. As we walk through these days together, we'll explore how the promises of Advent bring new light to our lives and deepen our awareness of Christ's presence. Each devotional will include a Scripture passage, a thoughtful reflection, and a prayer to help you intentionally draw closer to God as you prepare for the celebration of Christ's birth.

Easter Reflections: Celebrating the Resurrection

Easter is the pinnacle of our Christian faith—a day of victory and celebration as we honor the resurrection of Jesus Christ. Leading up to this profound event, Holy Week takes us through a journey of reflection, from the sorrow of Good Friday to the unimaginable joy of Resurrection Sunday. During this special series of Easter reflections, we'll remember the sacrifice Jesus made for us and the hope and redemption His resurrection brings.

These devotionals are designed to help you enter more fully into the mystery of the cross and the power of the empty tomb. Together, we will walk through key moments of Jesus' journey to the cross, reflect on the significance of His suffering, and rejoice in the new life we have through His resurrection. Each entry will provide a fresh perspective on God's love and grace, helping you to celebrate Easter with a renewed heart and a spirit filled with gratitude and hope.

"Peace I leave with you; My peace I give you. I do not give to you as the world gives. Do not let your hearts be troubled and do not be afraid."

John 14:27

Reflection: In what areas of your life do you need Christ's peace? How can you cultivate a heart that rests in His presence even when life feels uncertain?

Prayer: Prince of Peace, calm my anxious heart and fill me with Your peace. Let me become a vessel of Your peace to those around me, reflecting Your love in all I do.

"But the angel said to them, 'Do not be afraid. I bring you good news that will cause great joy for all the people. Today in the town of David a Savior has been born to you; He is the Messiah, the Lord.'"

Luke 2:10-11

Reflection: How can you embrace the joy of Christ's coming in your daily life? What practices can you incorporate this week to renew your sense

Christmas Reflections: The Gift of Emmanuel

Christmas is a season of wonder, joy, and the powerful reminder that God is with us. In these special Christmas reflections, we'll dive into the heart of the holiday, exploring the mystery and miracle of the Incarnation—God coming to earth in the form of a child. This is the season to reflect on God's extraordinary love, which sent His only Son to live among us, offering hope, salvation, and an invitation to live in communion with Him.

Each Christmas devotional will center on the beauty of the Christmas story, the humble setting of Christ's birth, and the impact of Emmanuel—God with us. Through Scripture, we'll revisit the awe of the shepherds, the faith of Mary, the journey of the Magi, and the transformative gift of Jesus. These reflections will guide you to see Christmas as more than a holiday; they'll help you to feel the warmth of God's love, the peace of His presence, and the joy of salvation. Let this Christmas be a time of spiritual renewal as we remember the true meaning of the season and celebrate the greatest gift of all.

Made in United States
Orlando, FL
06 December 2024

55097519R00134